IN or OUT?

EUROPE IN CARTOONS

Kipper Williams

AMBERLEY

For Pamela

A number of these cartoons originally appeared in the Guardian, the Spectator or Private Eye, so thanks to all concerned for allowing them to be used again here. Thanks also to E&T magazine (May 2016) for permission to re-use the cartoon on page 7.

This edition first published 2016

Amberley Publishing
The Hill, Stroud
Gloucestershire, GL5 4EP

www.amberley-books.com

British Library Cataloguing in Publication Data.
A catalogue record for this book is available from the British Library.

ISBN 978 1 4456 6282 4 (print)
ISBN 978 1 4456 6283 1 (ebook)

Typesetting and Origination by Amberley Publishing.
Printed in Great Britain.

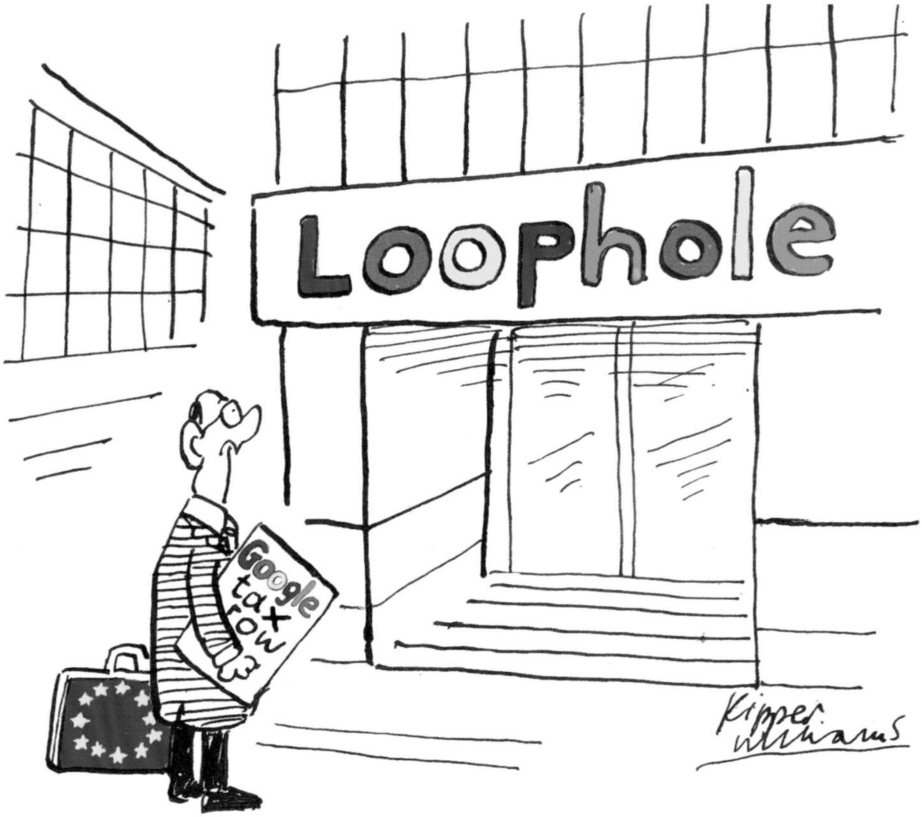
Loophole
Google tax row
Kipper Williams

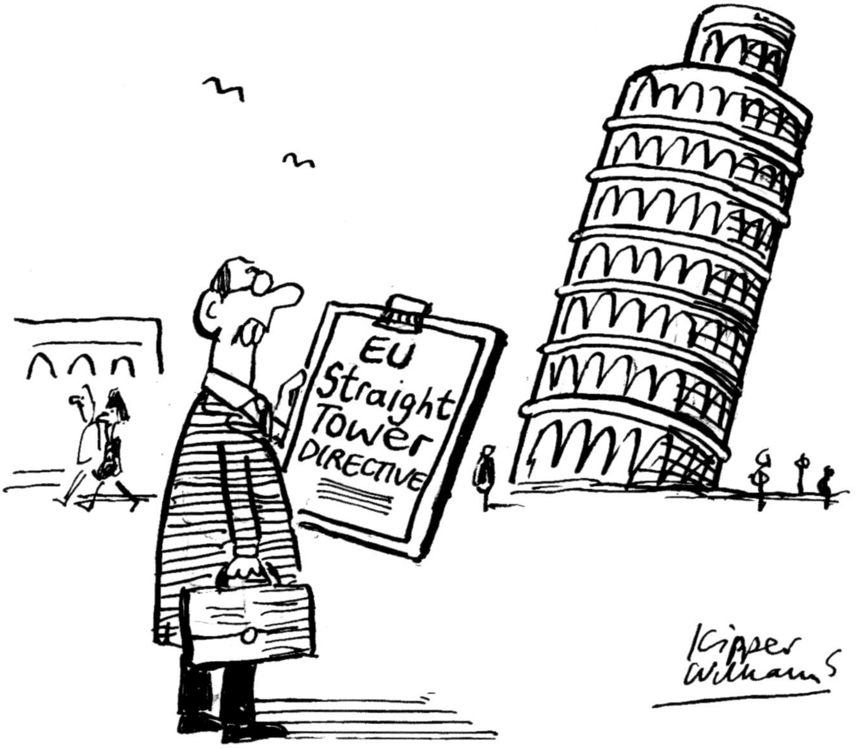
EU Straight Tower DIRECTIVE
Kipper Williams

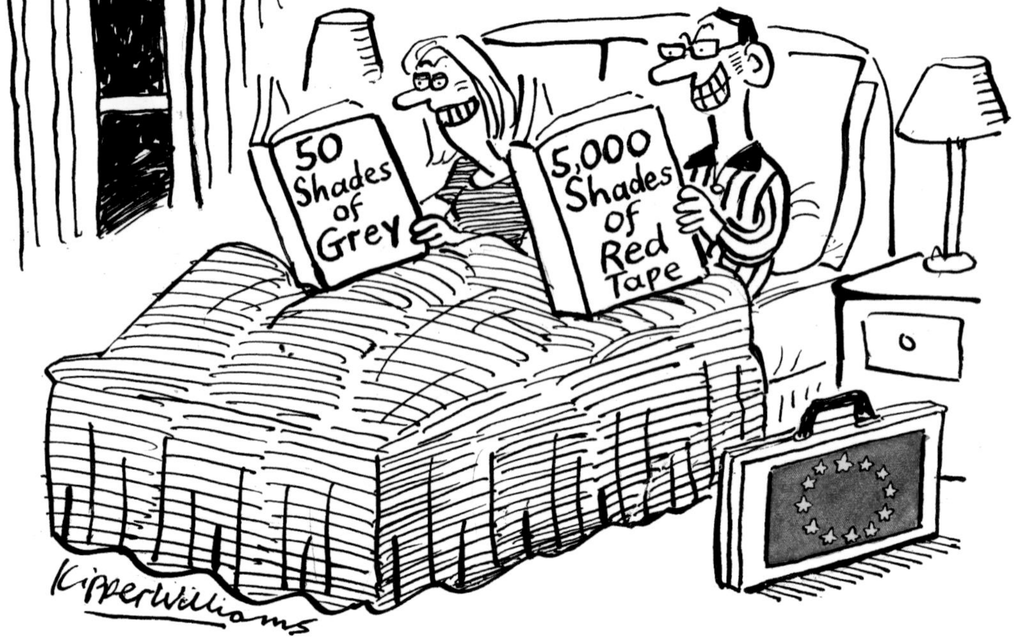
50 Shades of Grey
5,000 Shades of Red Tape
KipperWilliams

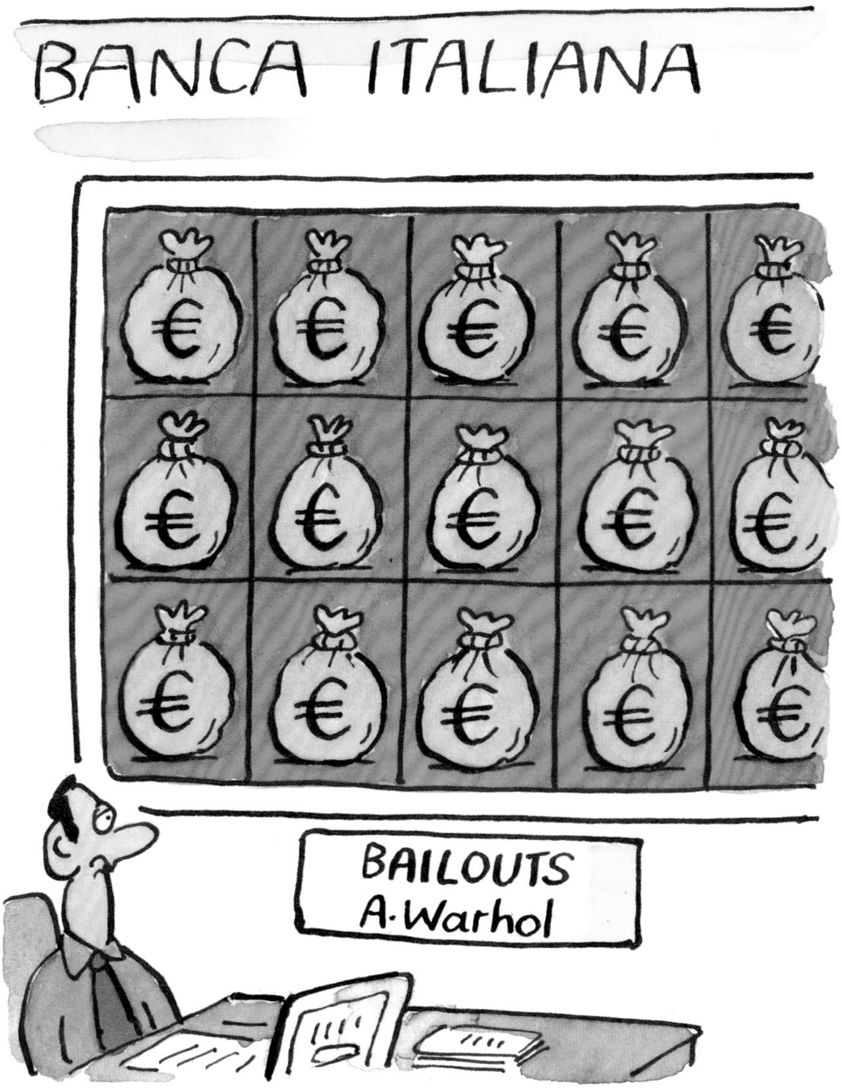
BANCA ITALIANA
BAILOUTS
A. Warhol

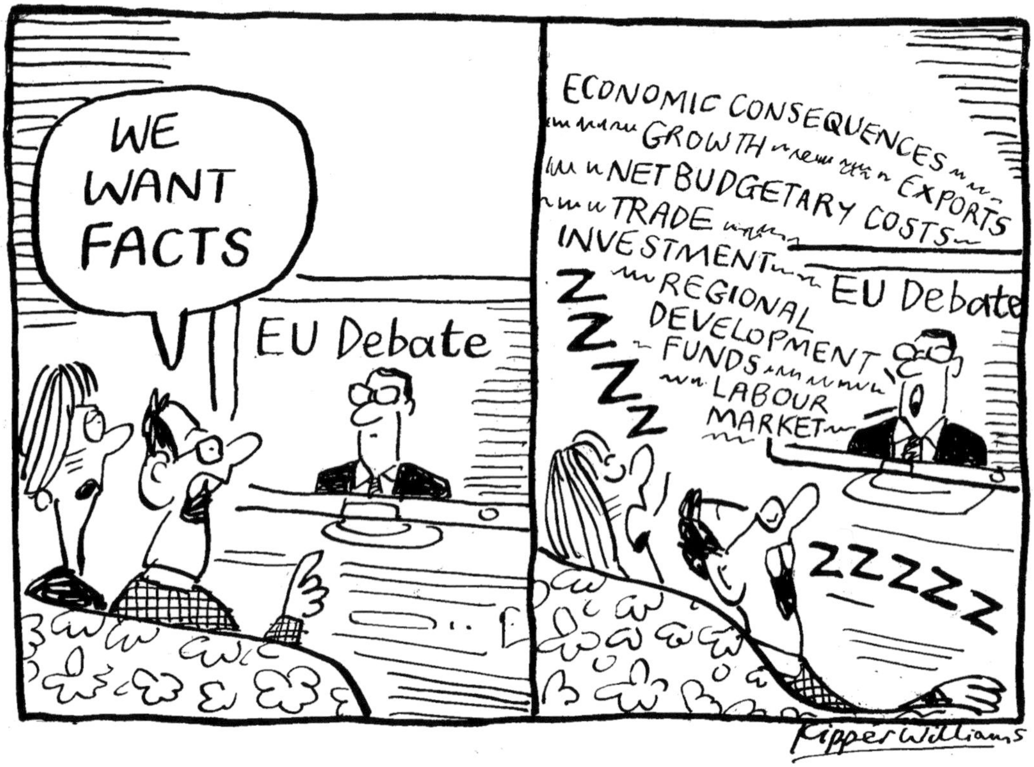
WE WANT FACTS
EU Debate
ECONOMIC CONSEQUENCES
GROWTH
NET BUDGETARY COSTS
EXPORTS
TRADE
INVESTMENT
REGIONAL DEVELOPMENT FUNDS
LABOUR MARKET
EU Debate
ZZZZ
ZZZZZ
Kipper Williams

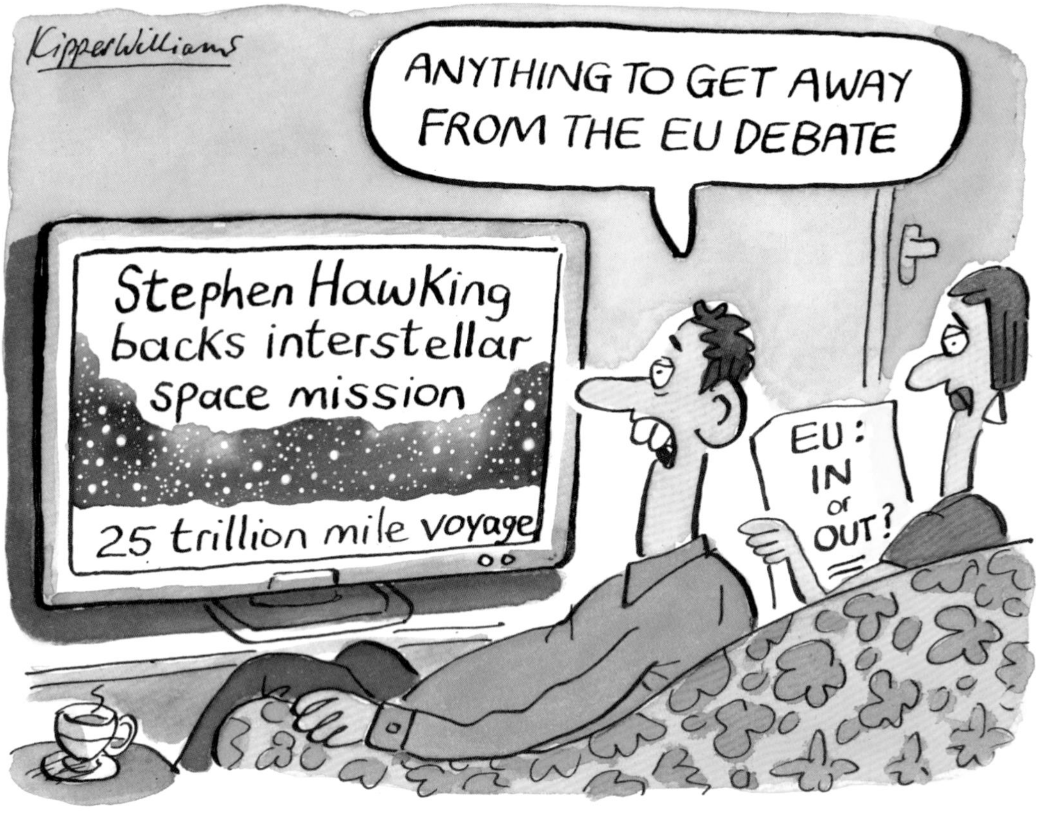
KipperWilliams
ANYTHING TO GET AWAY FROM THE EU DEBATE
Stephen Hawking backs interstellar space mission
25 trillion mile voyage
EU: IN or OUT?

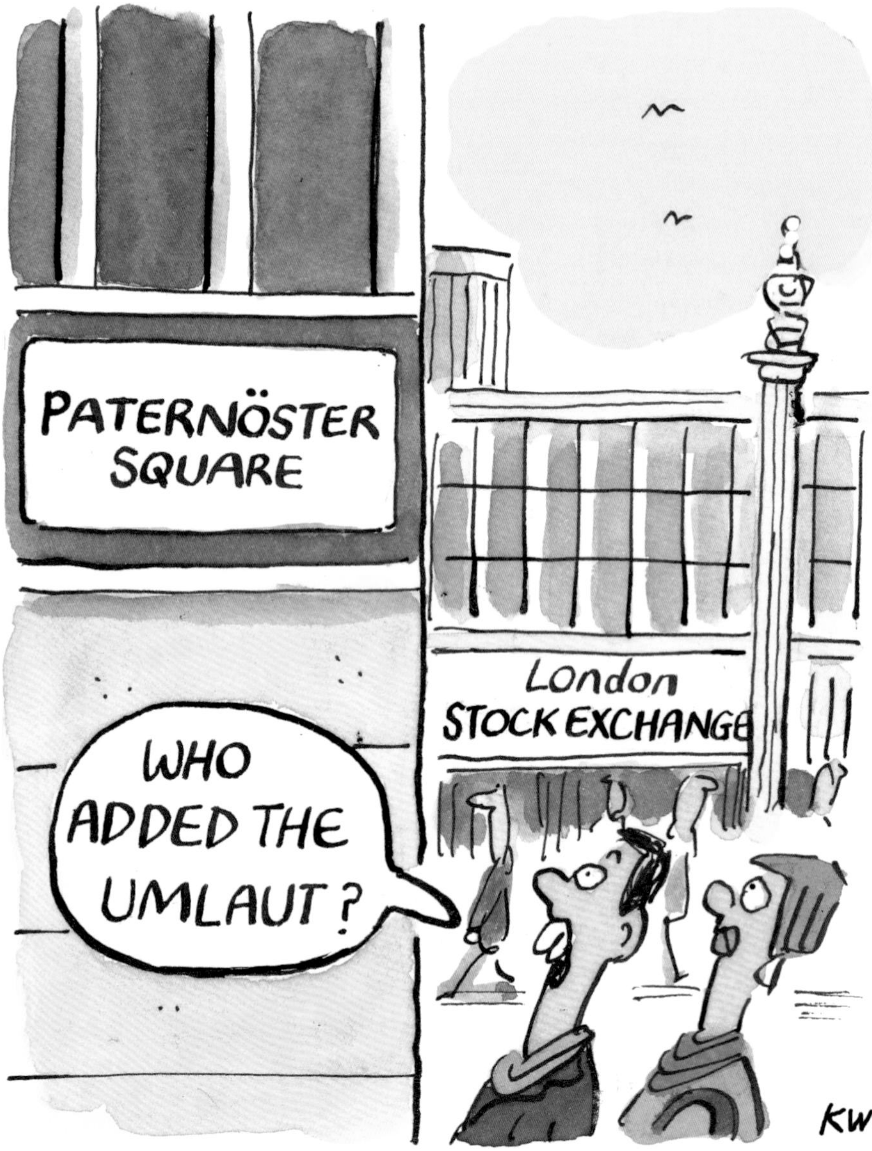
PATERNÖSTER
SQUARE
London
STOCK EXCHANGE
WHO
ADDED THE
UMLAUT ?
KW

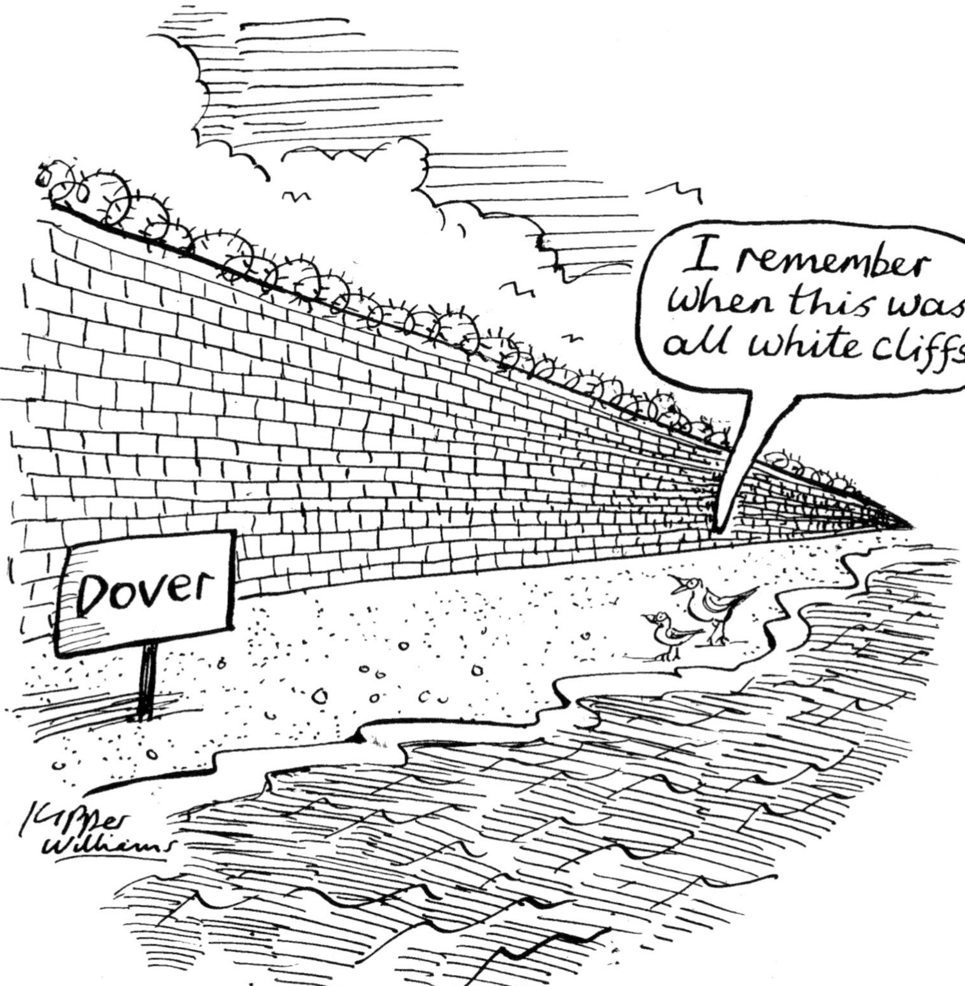
I remember when this was all white cliffs
Dover
Kipper Williams

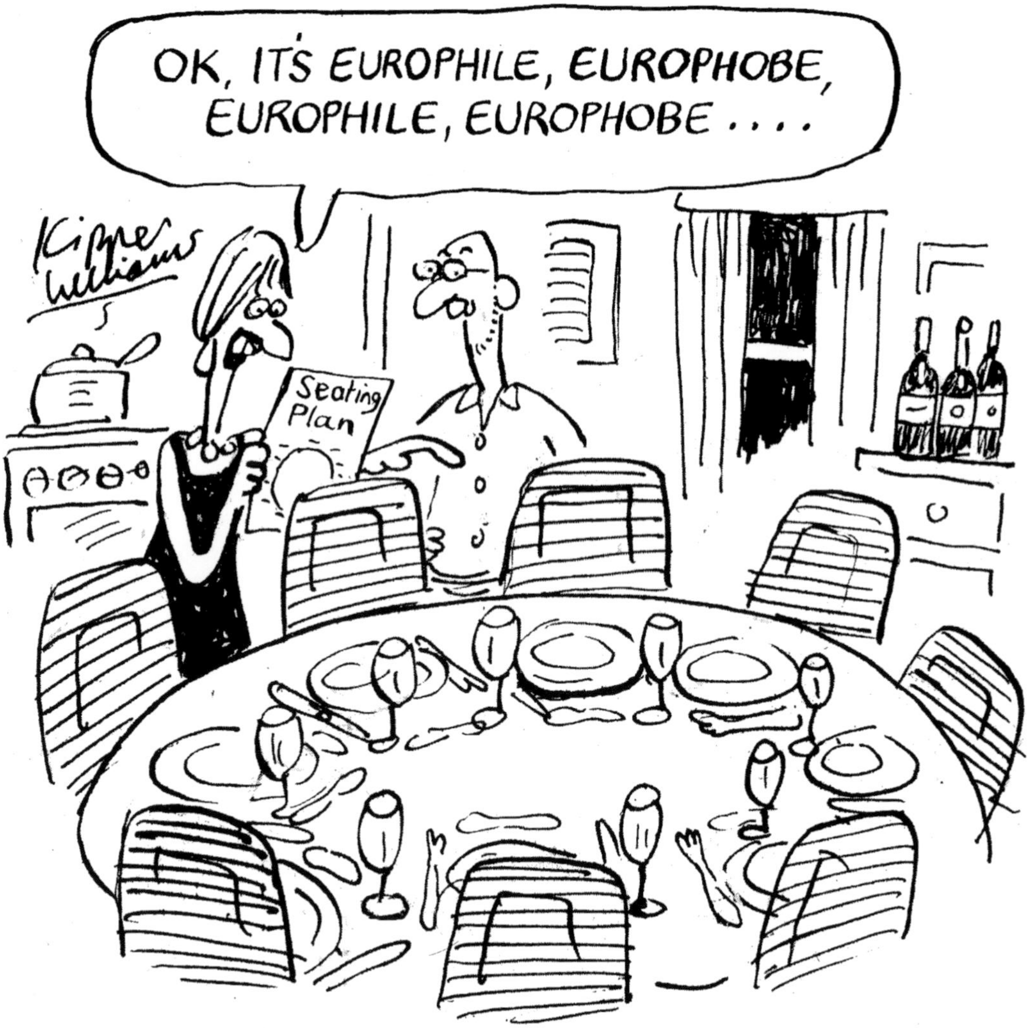
OK, IT'S EUROPHILE, EUROPHOBE, EUROPHILE, EUROPHOBE . . . .
Seating Plan
Kipper Williams

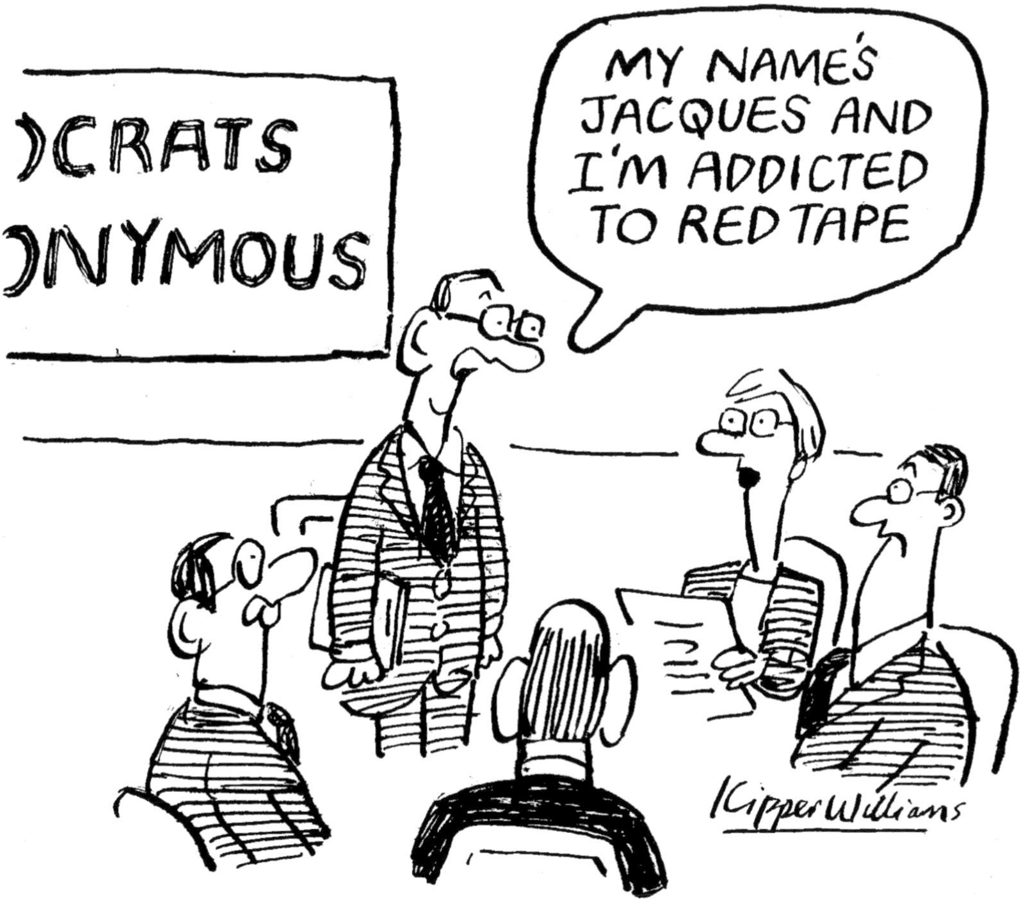
MY NAME'S JACQUES AND I'M ADDICTED TO RED TAPE
)CRATS
)NYMOUS
Kipper Williams

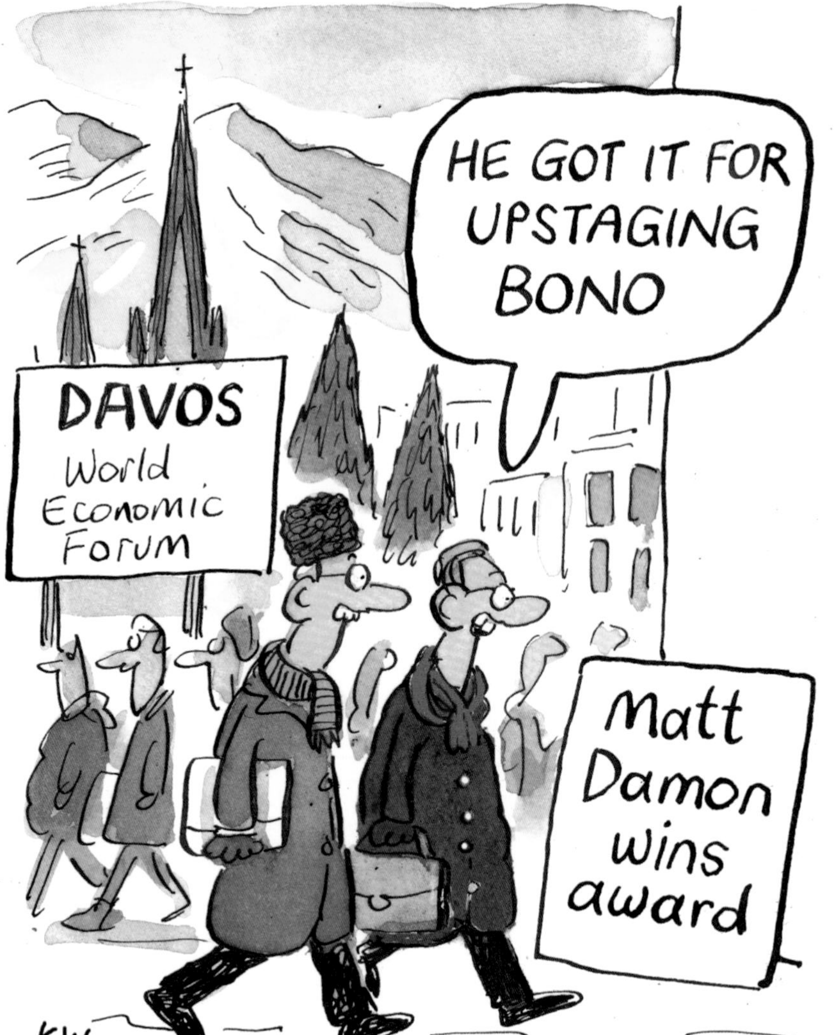
HE GOT IT FOR UPSTAGING BONO
DAVOS
World Economic Forum
Matt Damon wins award
KW

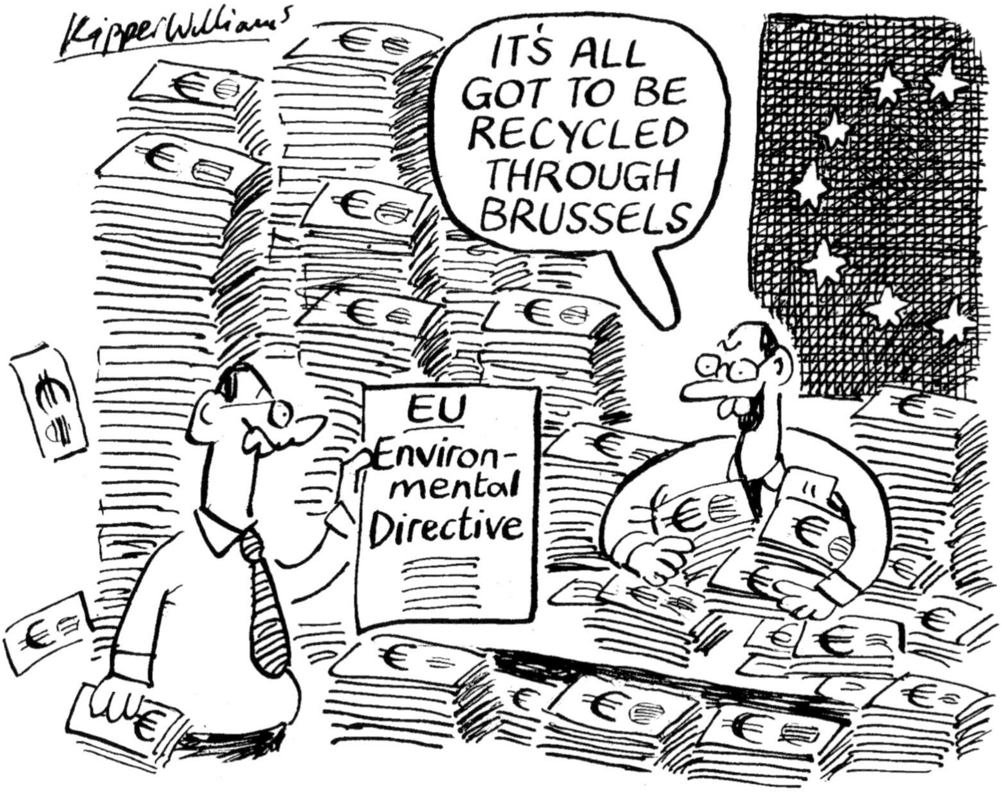
Kipper Williams
IT'S ALL GOT TO BE RECYCLED THROUGH BRUSSELS
EU Environmental Directive

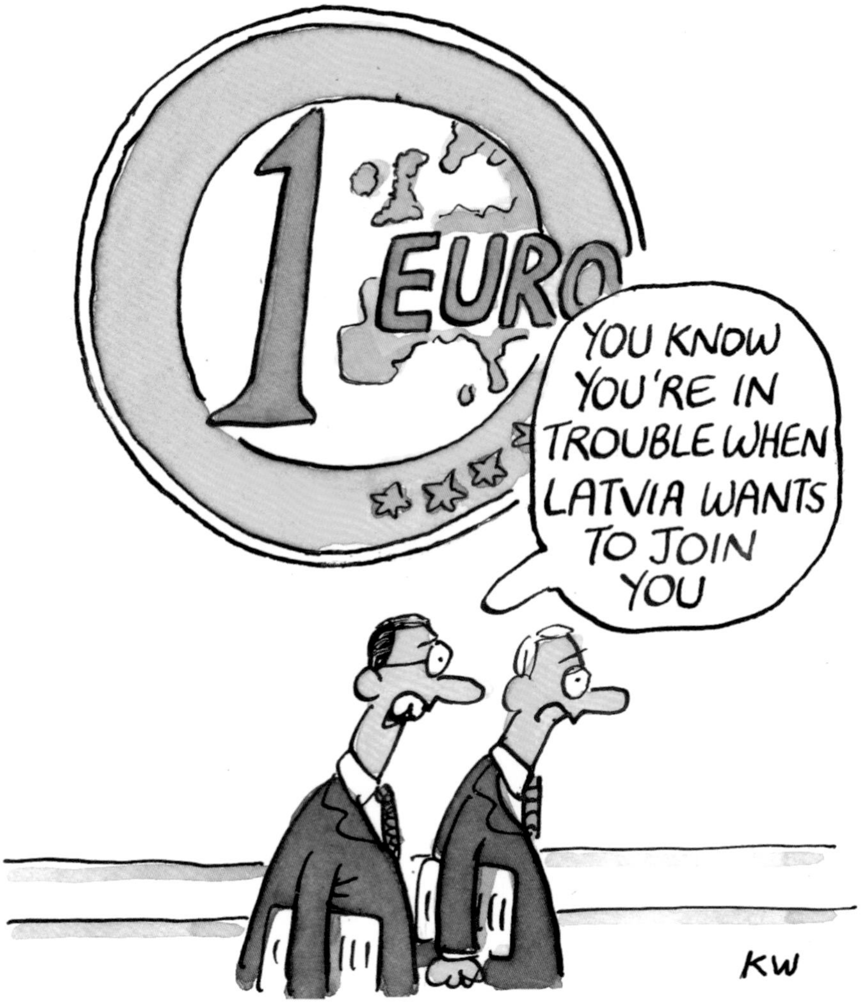
1
EURO
YOU KNOW YOU'RE IN TROUBLE WHEN LATVIA WANTS TO JOIN YOU
KW

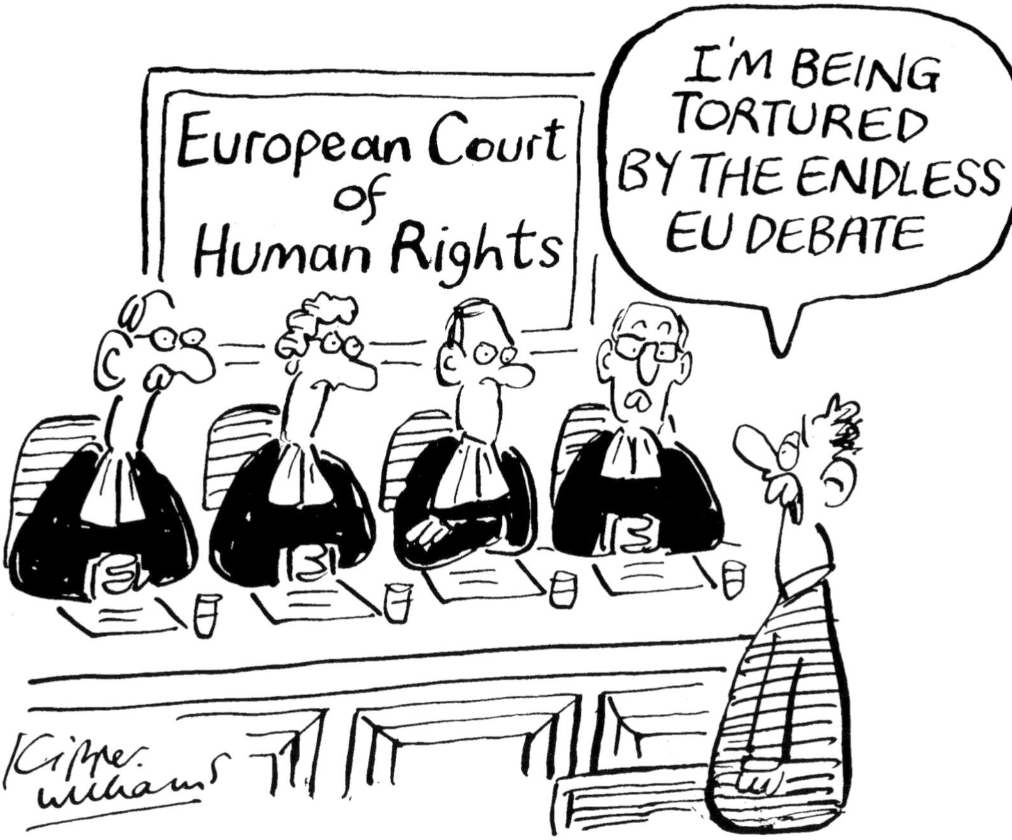
European Court of Human Rights
I'M BEING TORTURED BY THE ENDLESS EU DEBATE
Kipper Williams

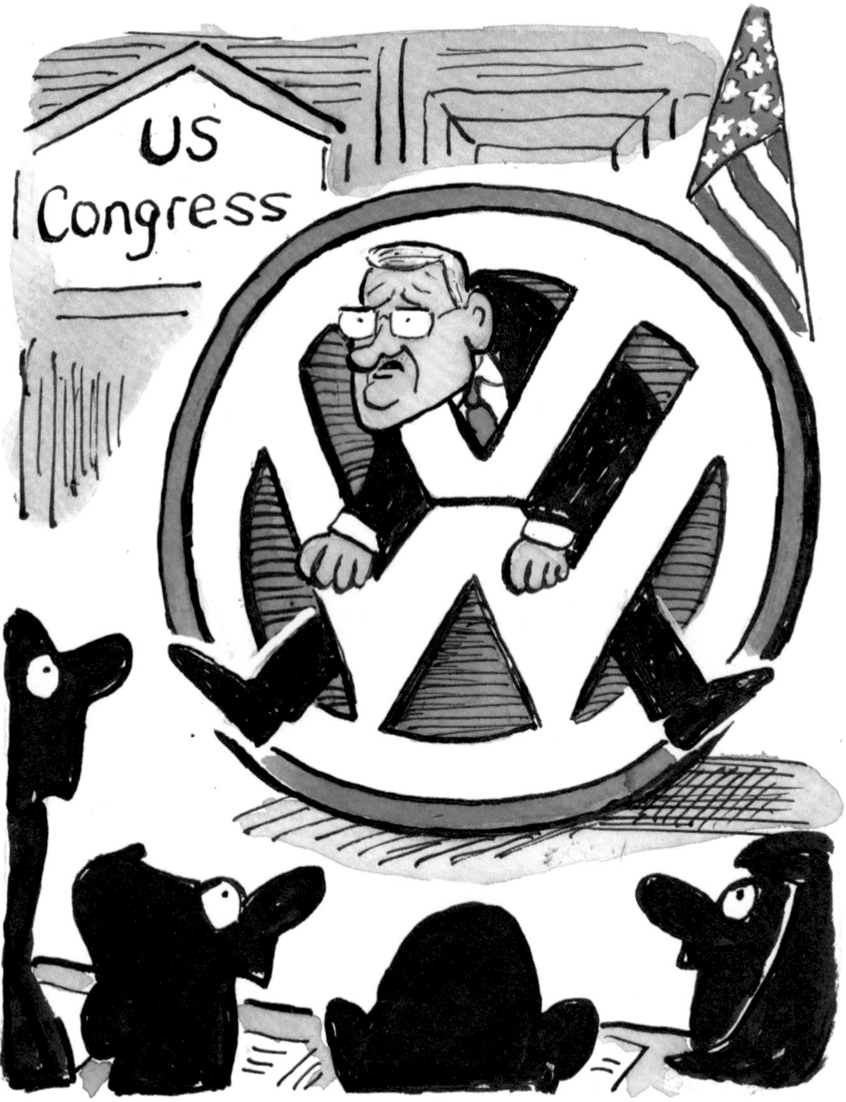
US
Congress

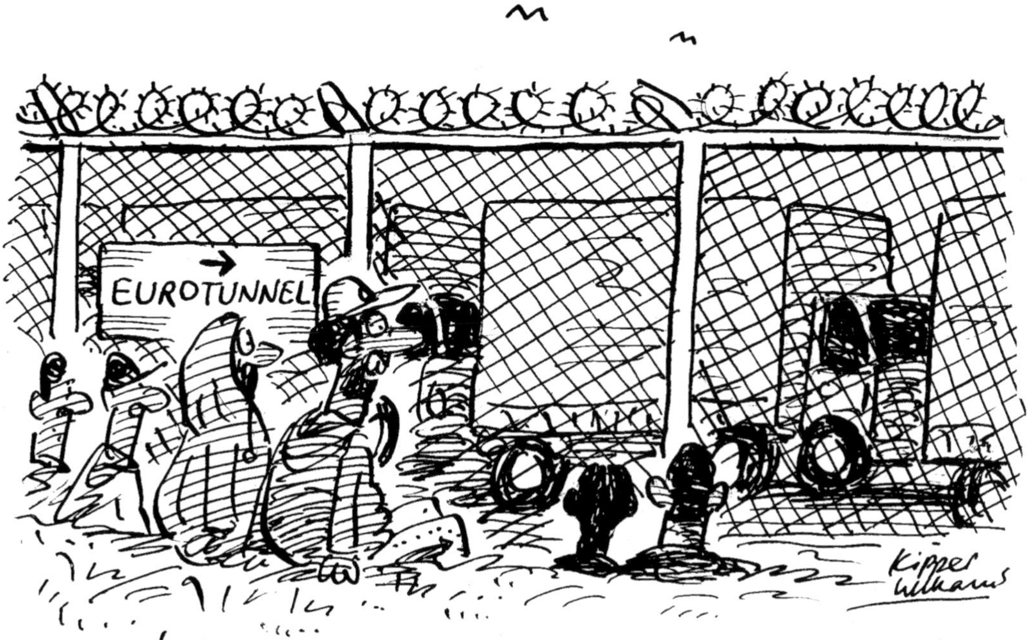
EUROTUNNEL
Kipper Williams

'I only want to get to the UK to annoy Nigel Farage.'

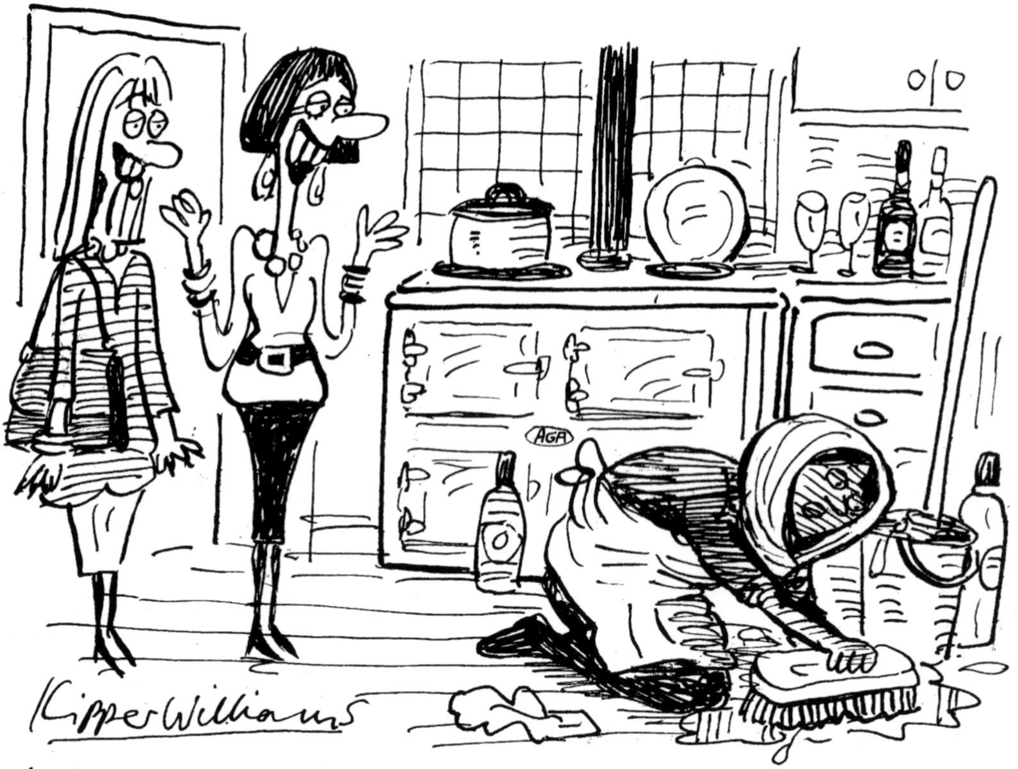
AGA

'Our asylum seeker's an absolute treasure.'

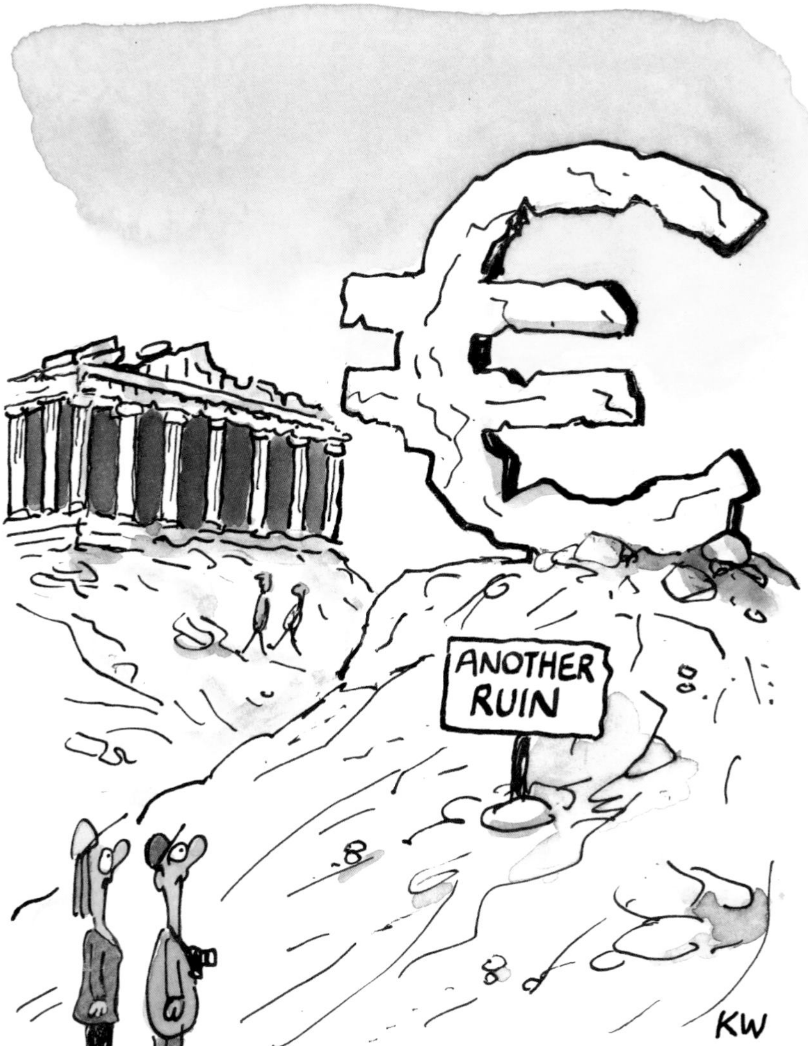
ANOTHER
RUIN
KW

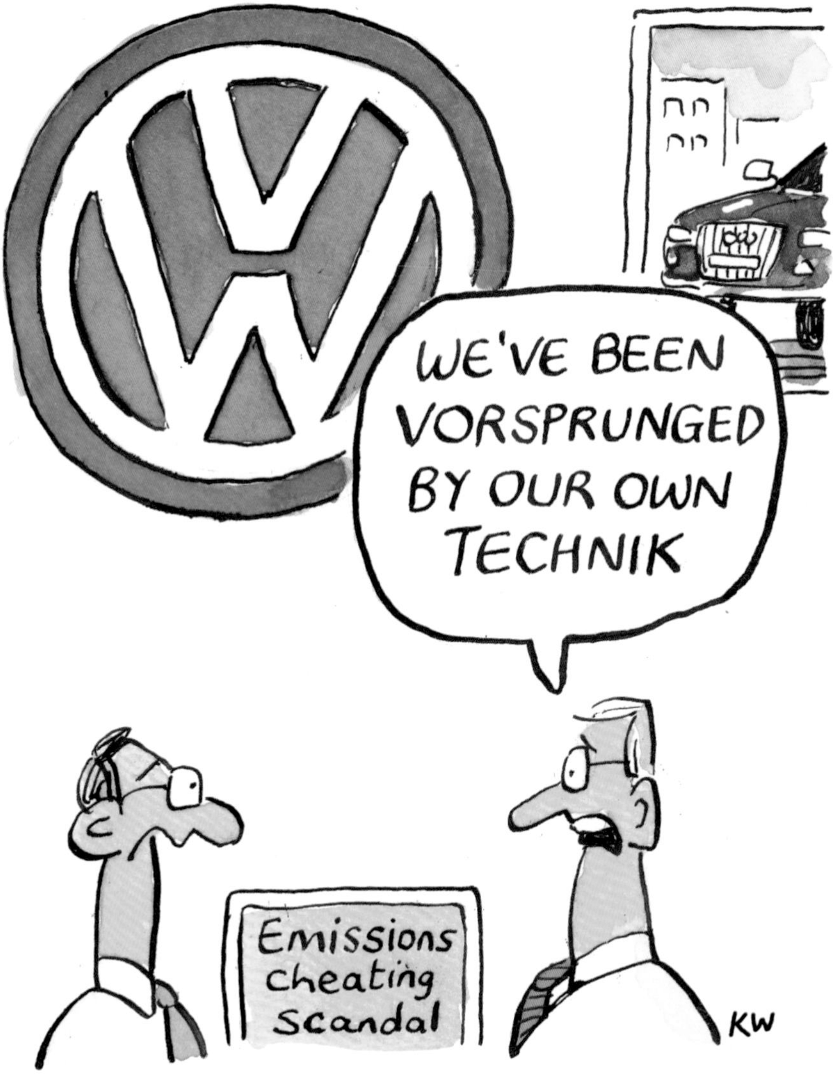
WE'VE BEEN VORSPRUNGED BY OUR OWN TECHNIK
Emissions cheating scandal
KW

eDF ENERGY
Hinkley Point
NUCLEAR POWER STATION
Project
WE OUGHT
TO THINK
TWICE
KipperWilliams

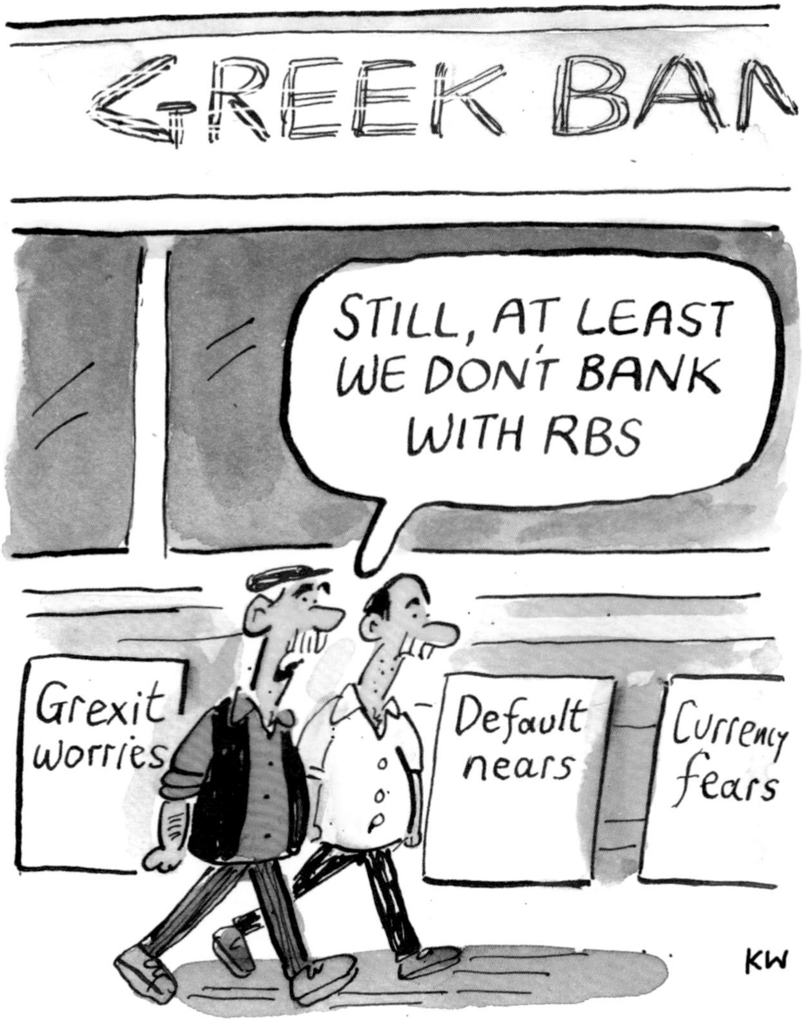
GREEK BAN
STILL, AT LEAST WE DON'T BANK WITH RBS
Grexit worries
Default nears
Currency fears
KW

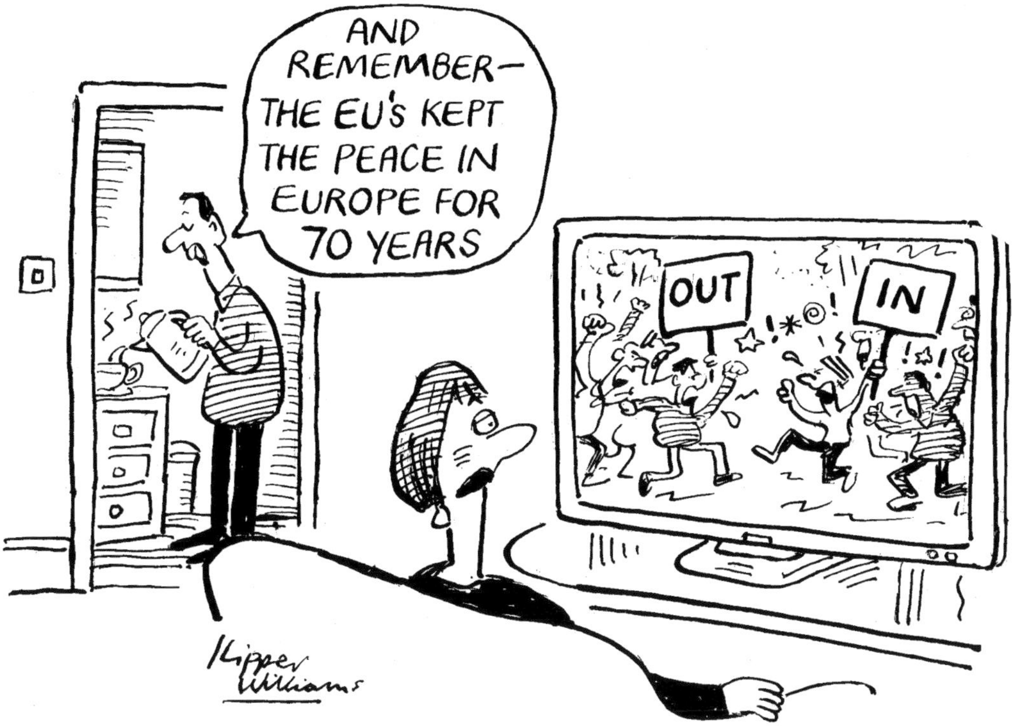
AND REMEMBER— THE EU'S KEPT THE PEACE IN EUROPE FOR 70 YEARS
OUT
IN
Kipper Williams

Groundhog Day

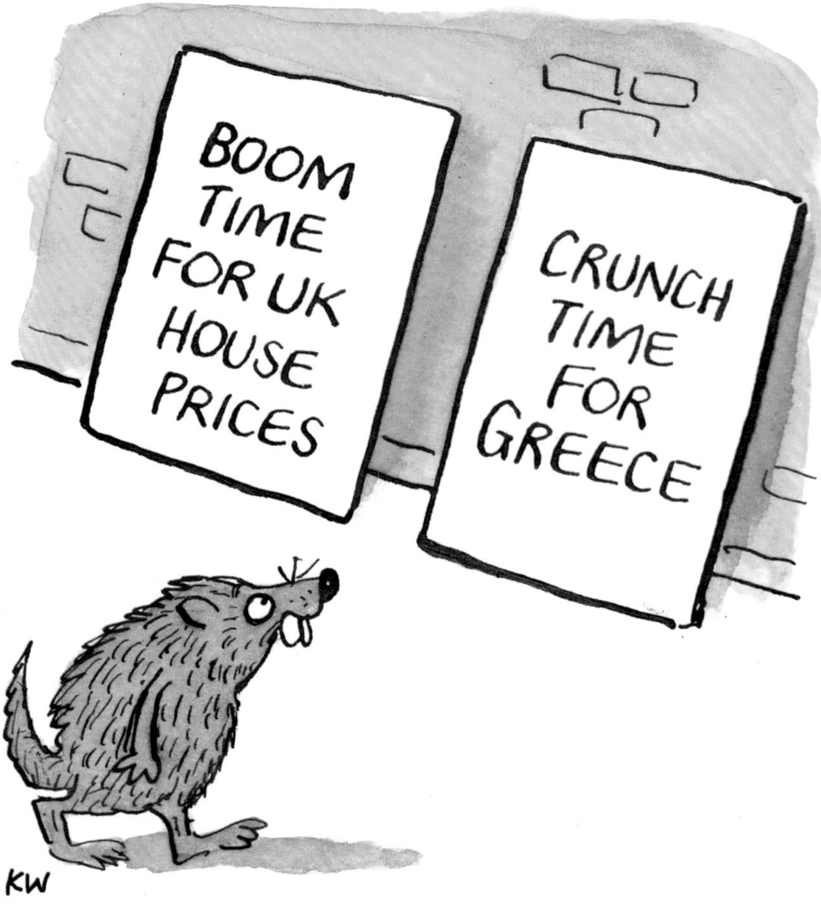
BOOM TIME FOR UK HOUSE PRICES
CRUNCH TIME FOR GREECE
KW

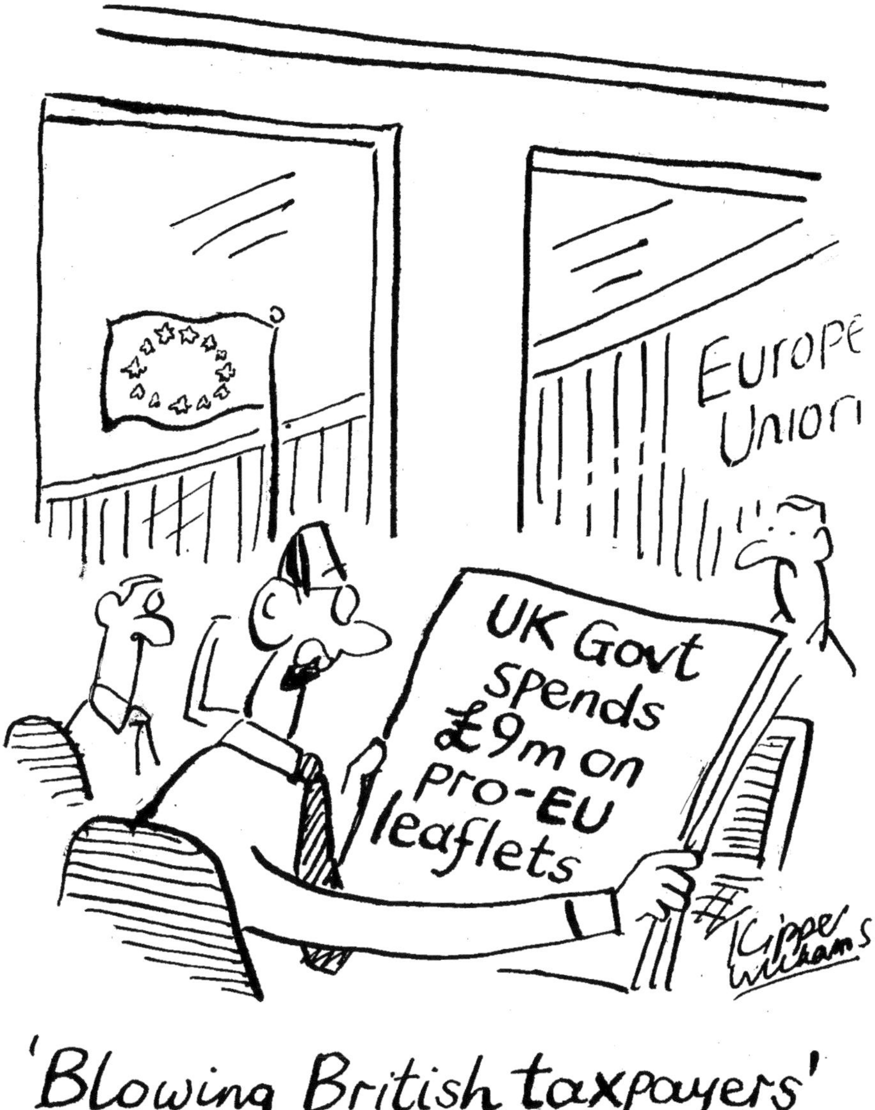
Europe
Union
UK Govt spends £9m on pro-EU leaflets
Kipper Williams

'Blowing British taxpayers' money? That's our job!'

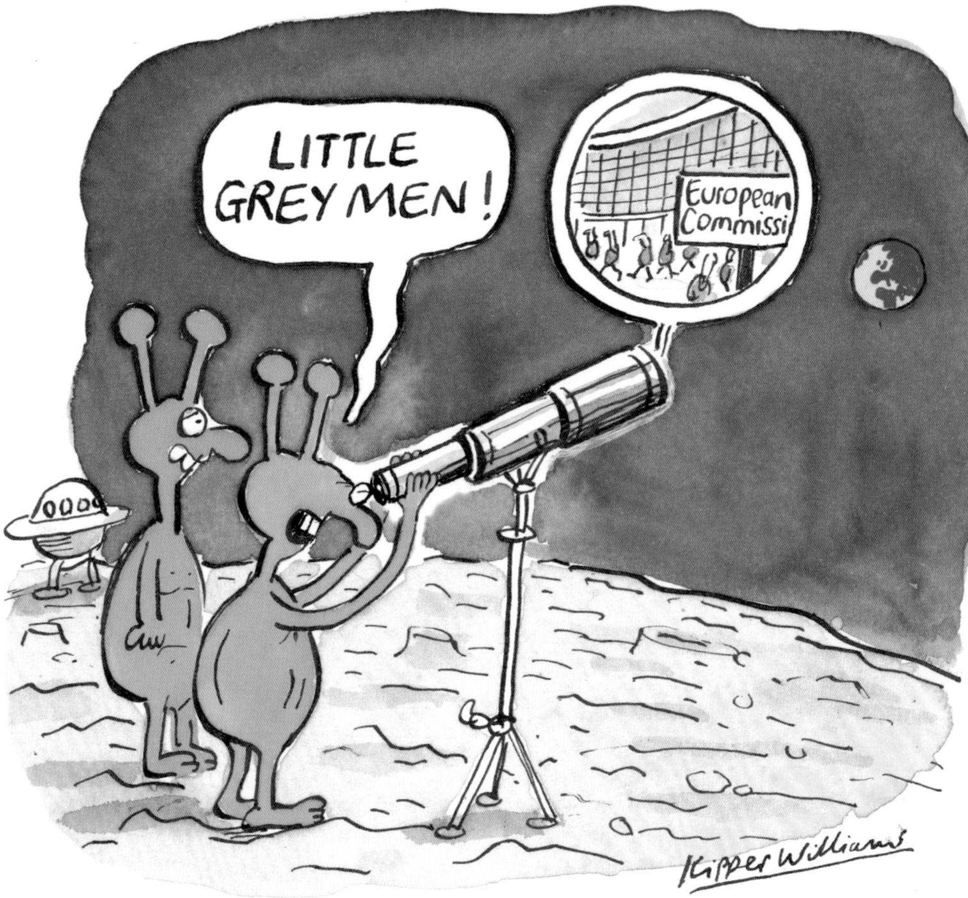
LITTLE GREY MEN!
European Commissi
Kipper Williams

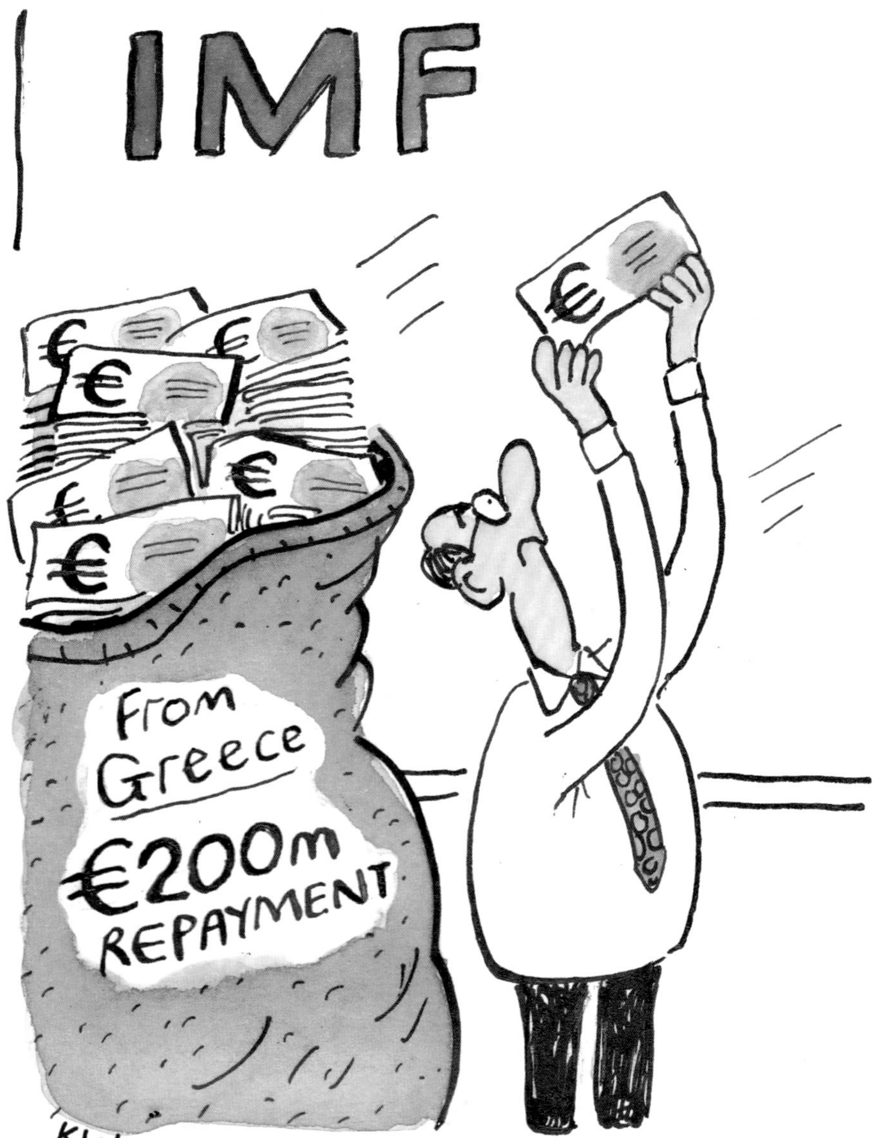
IMF
From Greece
€200m REPAYMENT
KW

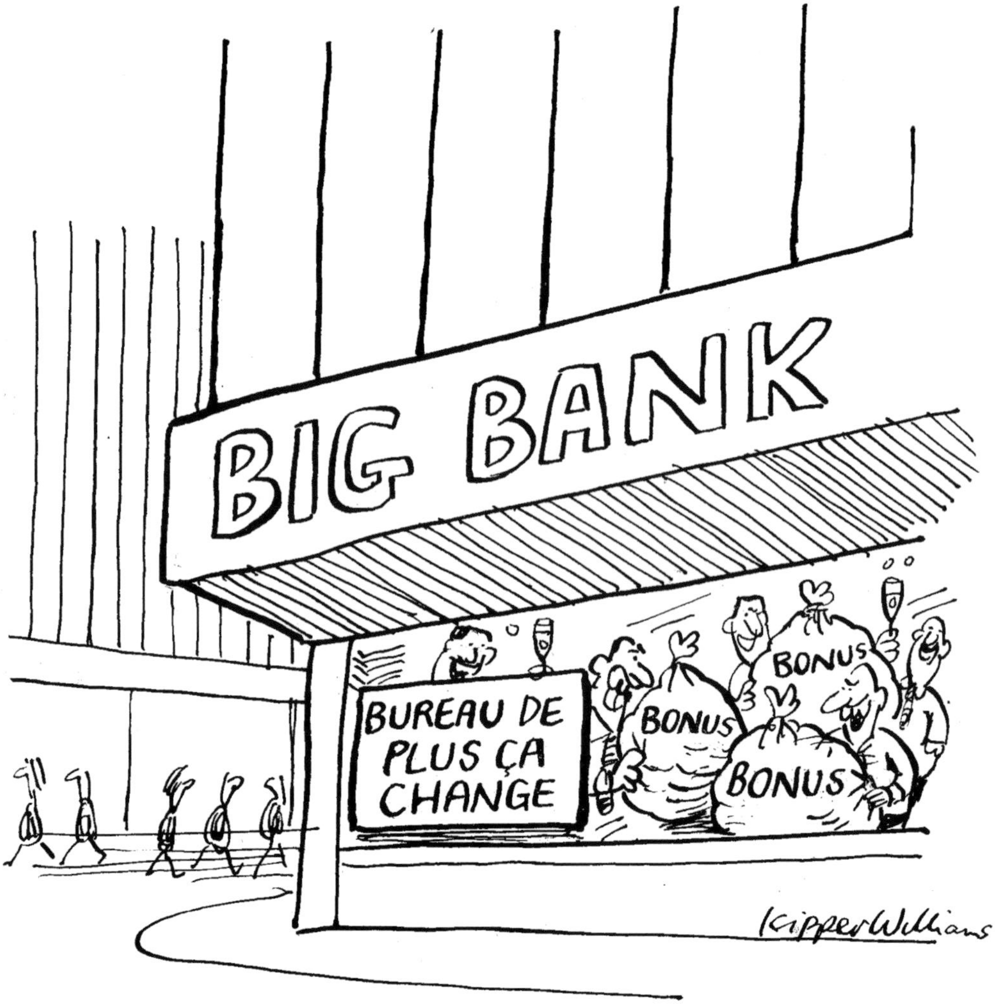
BIG BANK
BUREAU DE PLUS ÇA CHANGE
BONUS
BONUS
BONUS
KipperWilliams

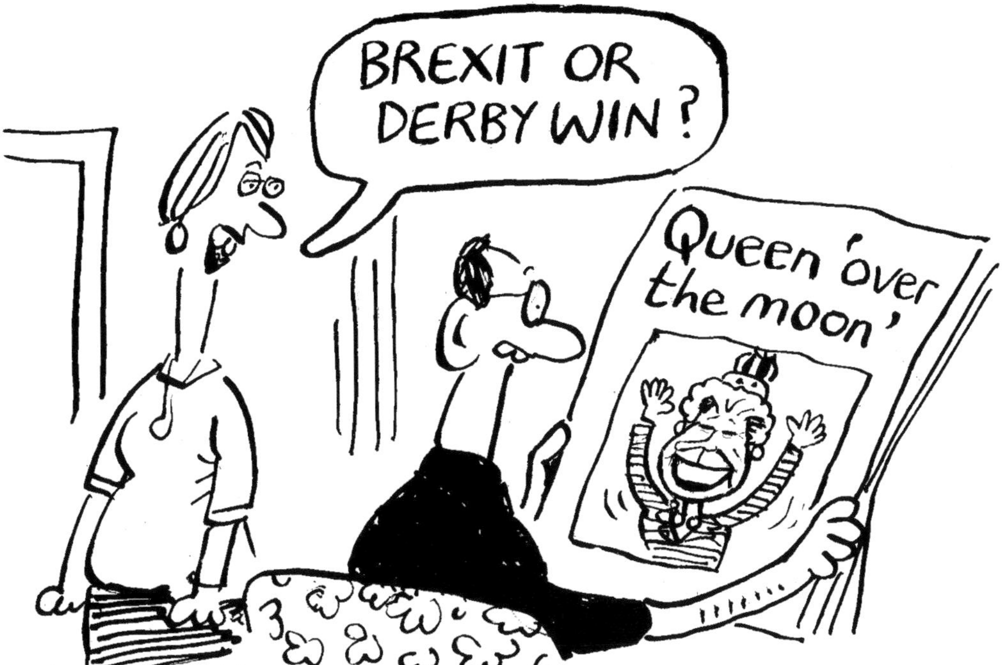
BREXIT OR DERBY WIN?
Queen 'over the moon'
KipperWilliams

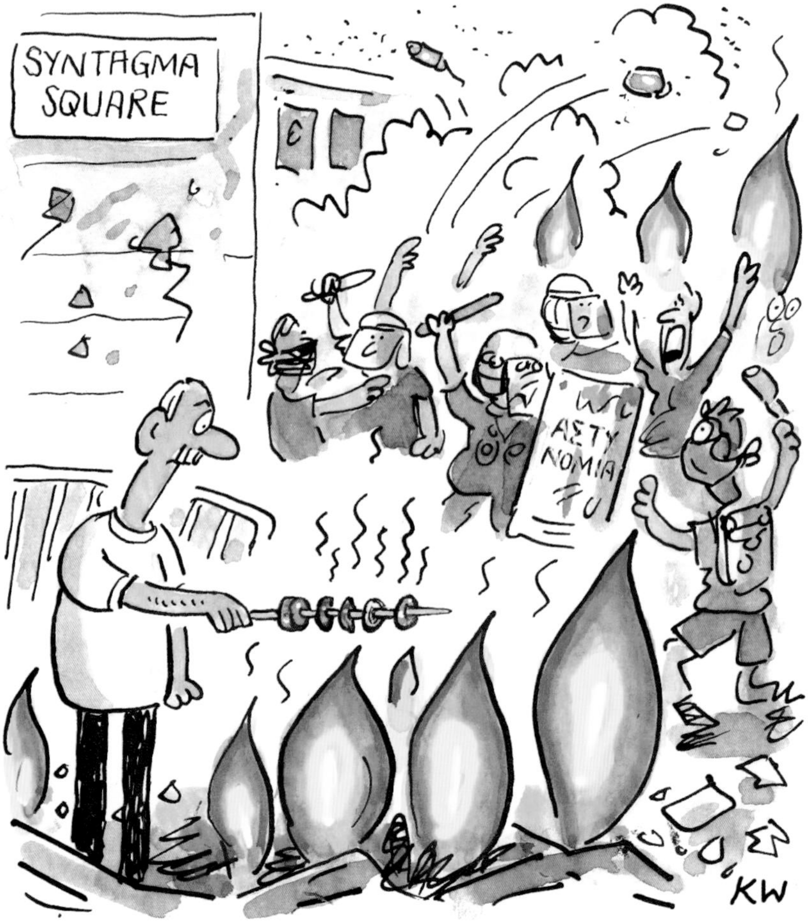
SYNTAGMA
SQUARE
ΑΣΤΥ
NOMIA
KW

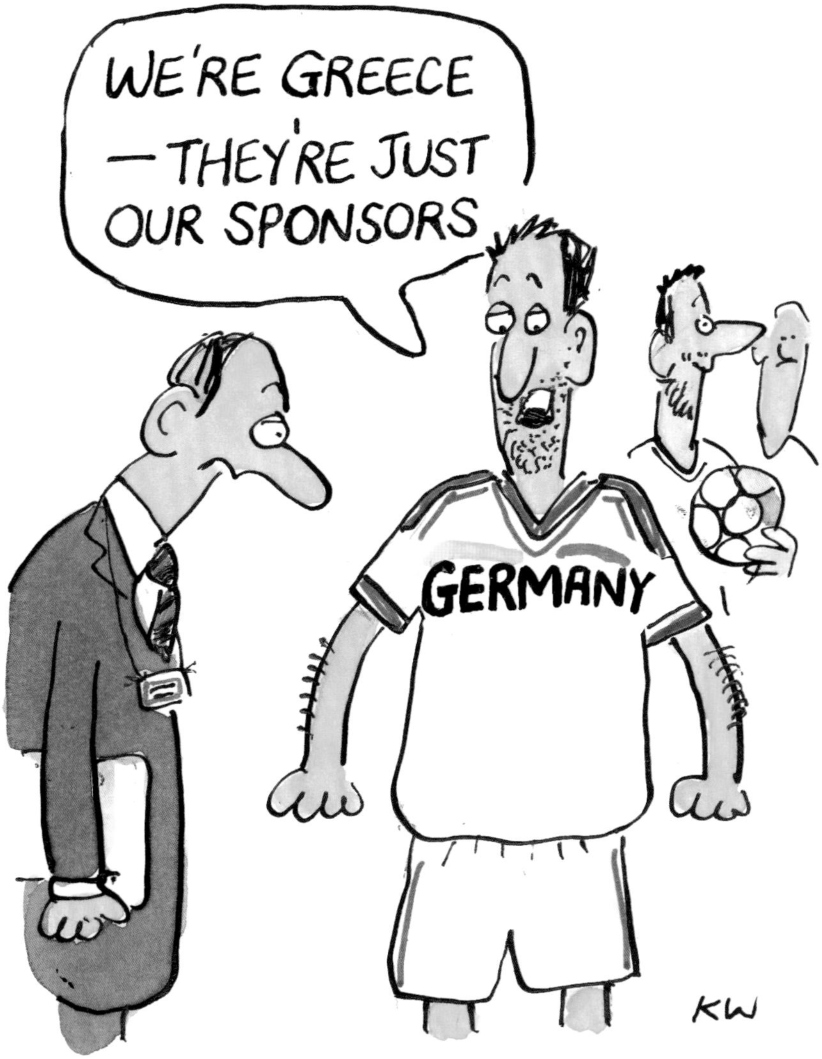
WE'RE GREECE — THEY'RE JUST OUR SPONSORS
GERMANY
KW

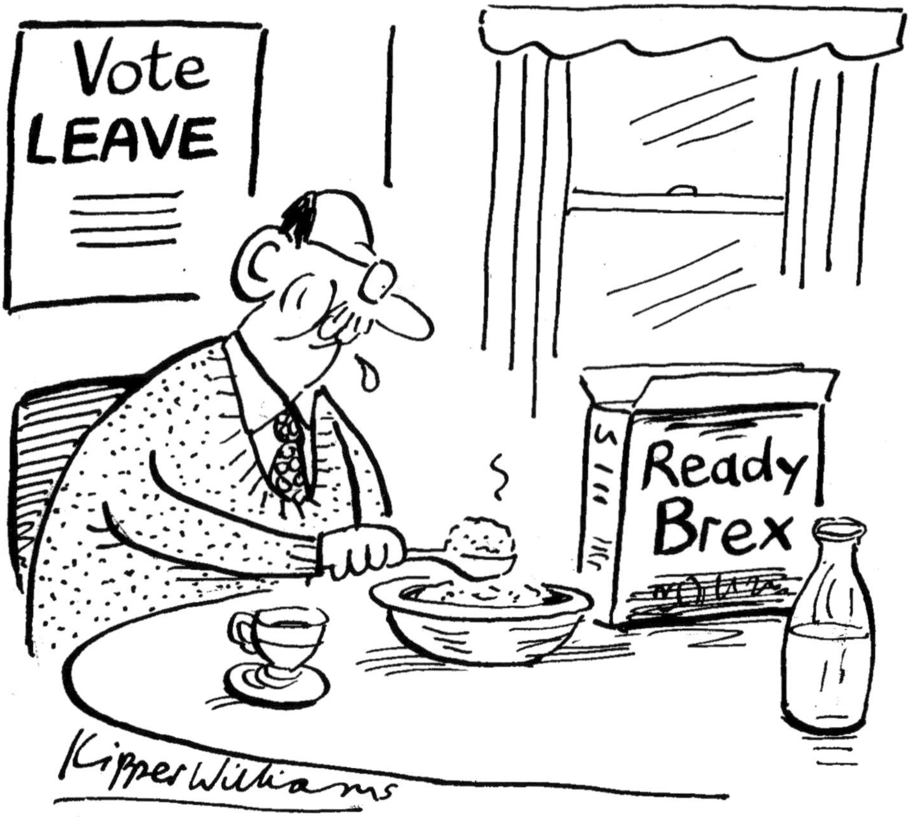
Vote
LEAVE
Ready
Brex
Kipper Williams

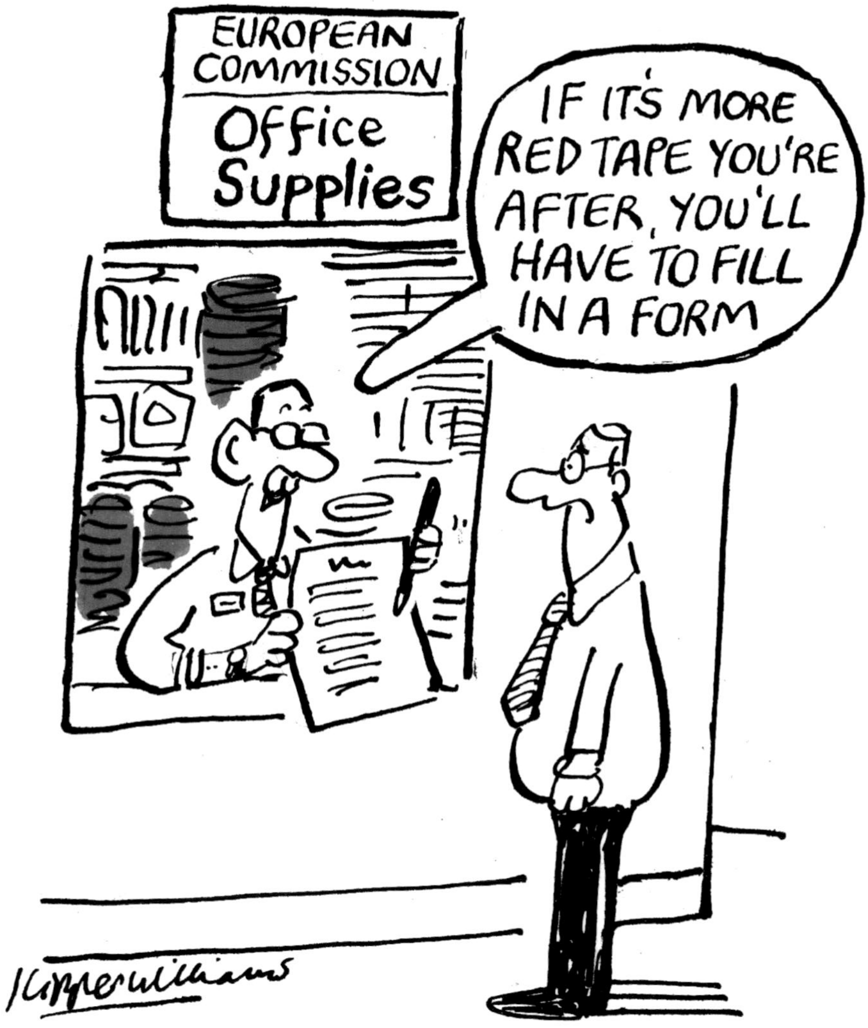
EUROPEAN COMMISSION
Office Supplies
IF IT'S MORE RED TAPE YOU'RE AFTER, YOU'LL HAVE TO FILL IN A FORM

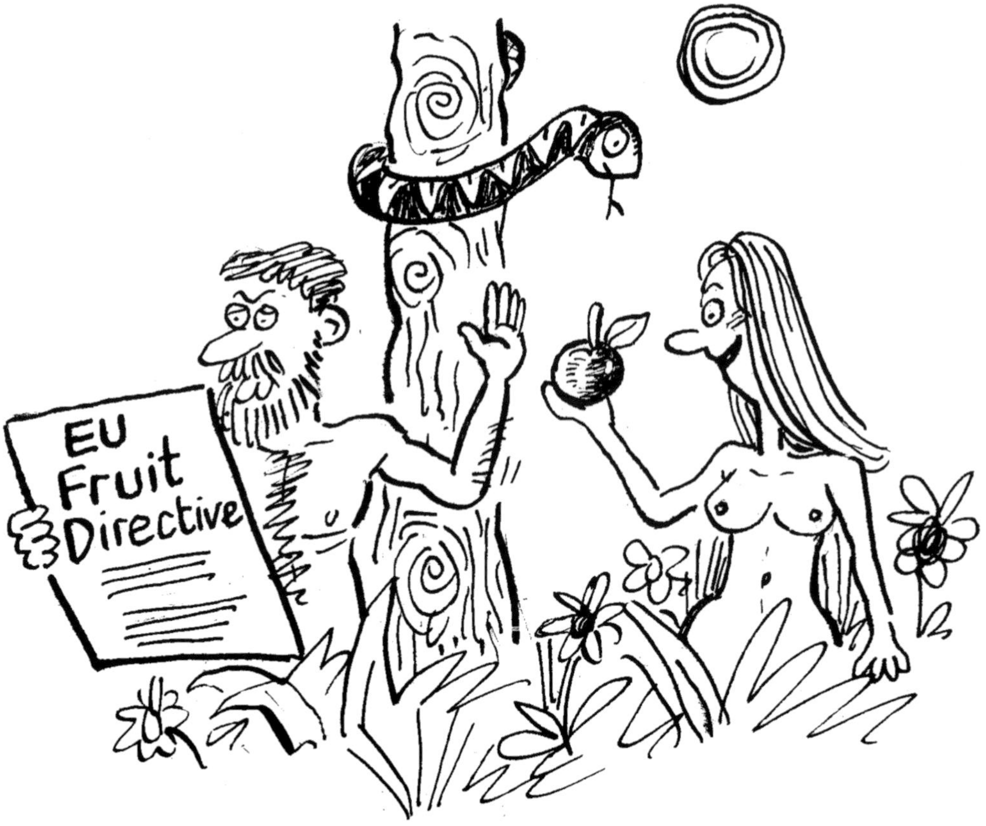
EU
Fruit
Directive

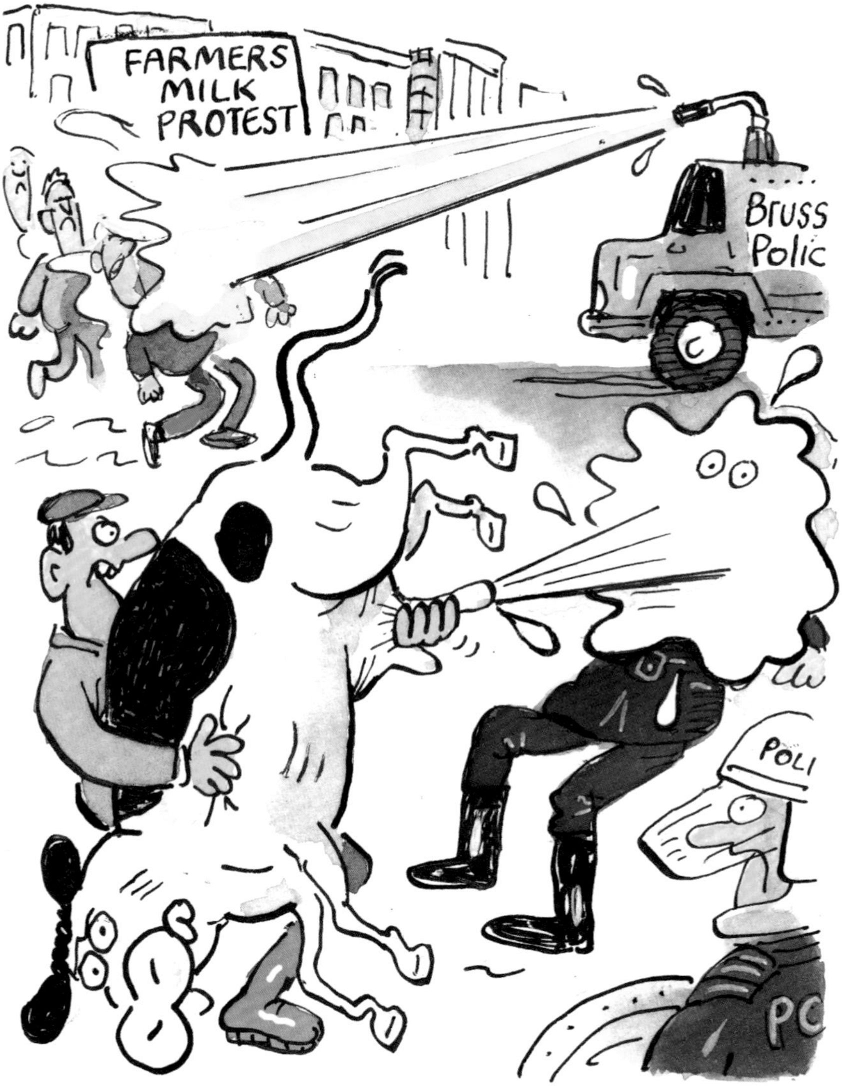
FARMERS
MILK
PROTEST
Bruss
Polic
POLI
PO

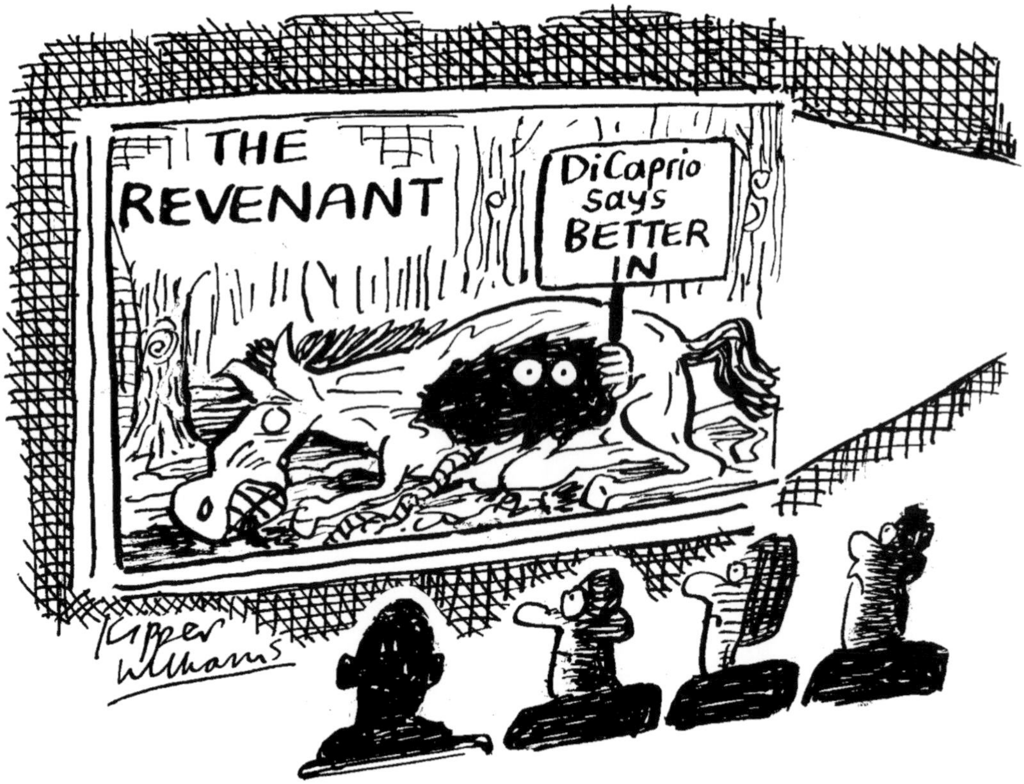
THE REVENANT
DiCaprio says BETTER IN
Kipper Williams

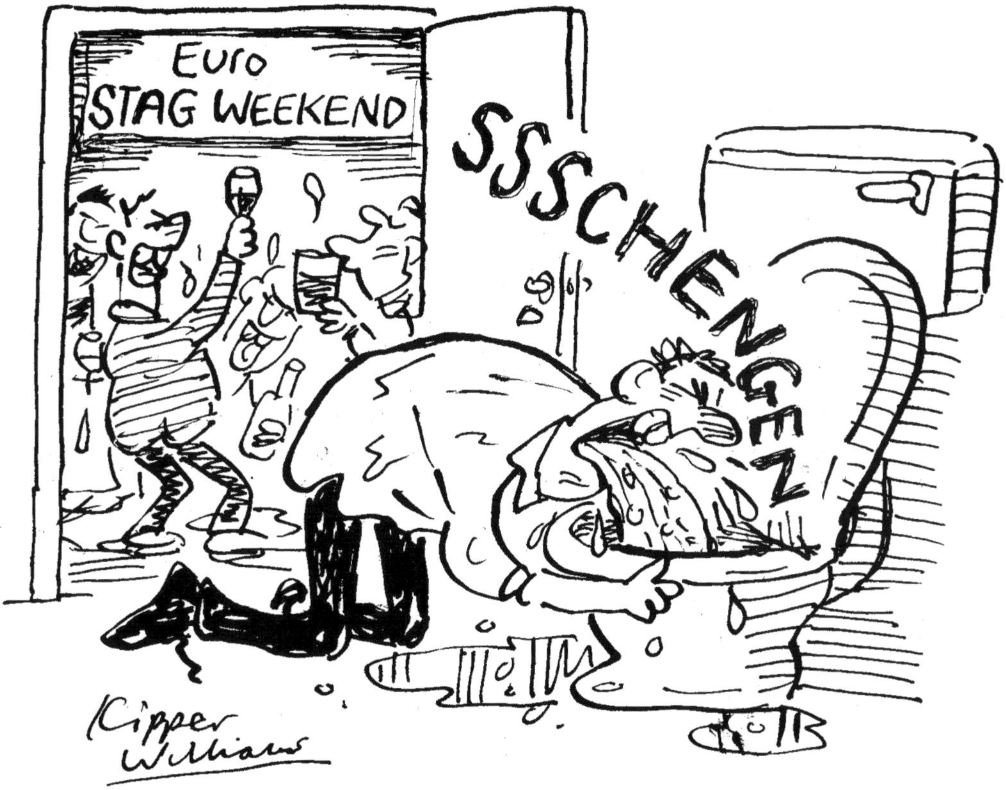
Euro
STAG WEEKEND
SSSCHENGEN
Kipper Williams

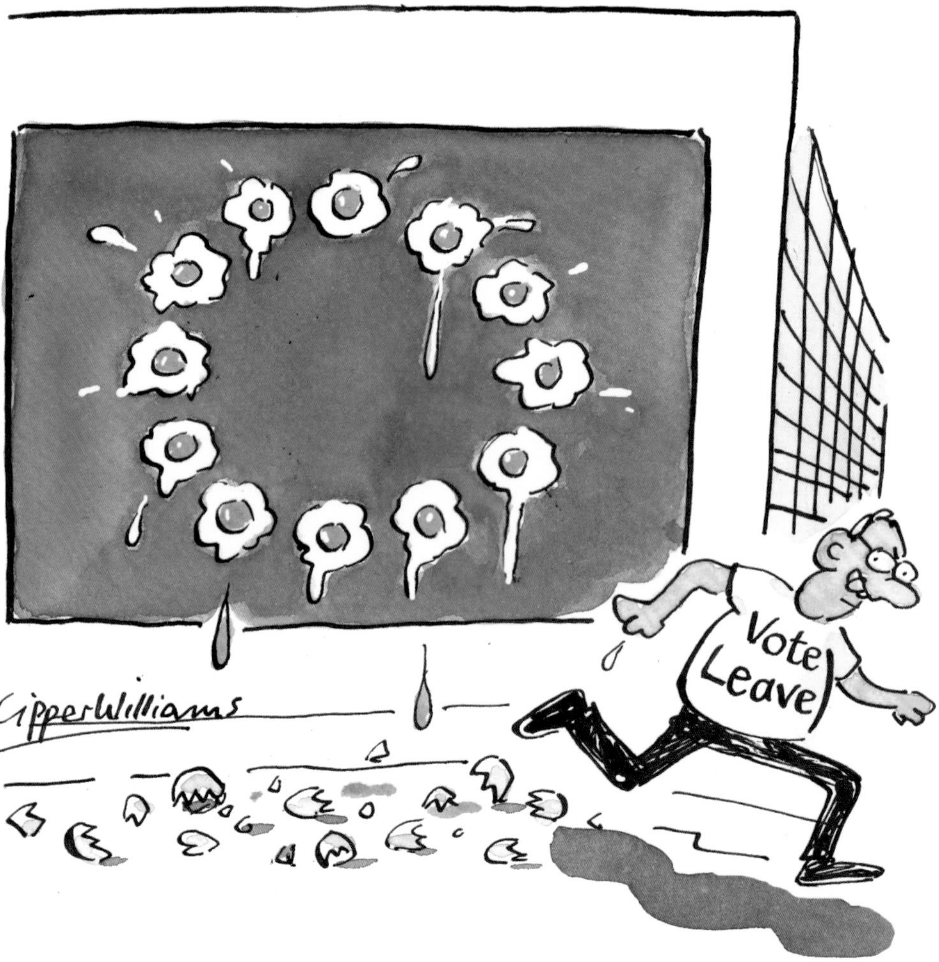
KipperWilliams
Vote
Leave

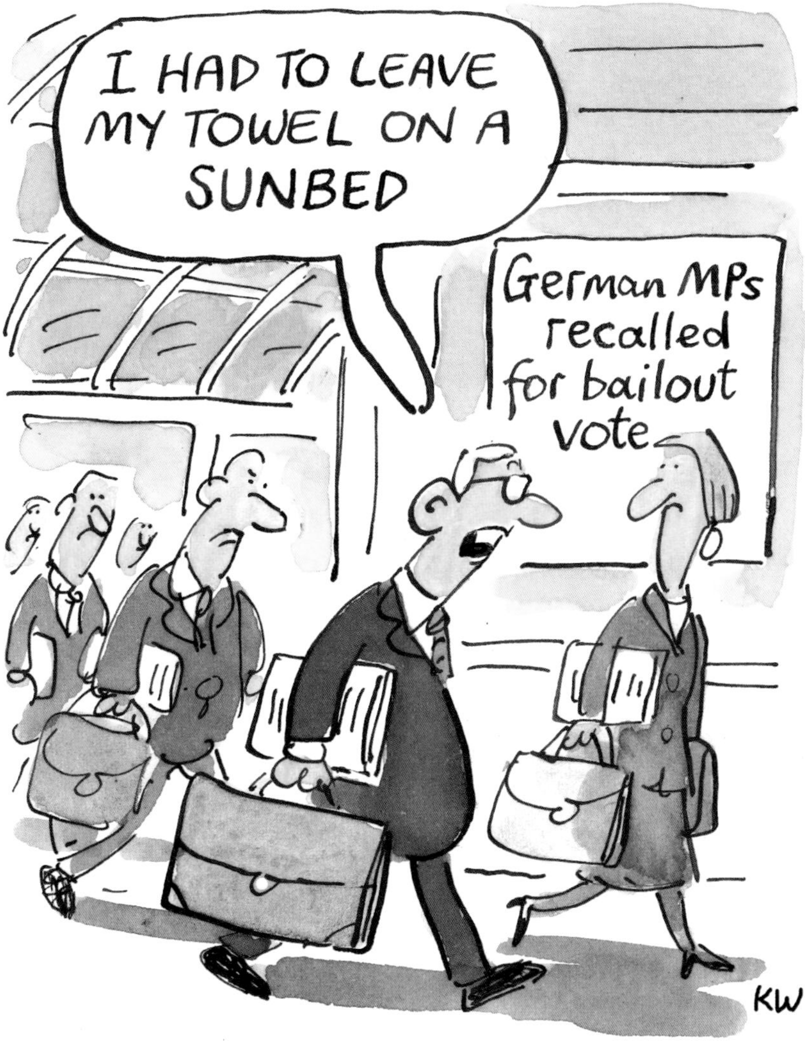
I HAD TO LEAVE MY TOWEL ON A SUNBED
German MPs recalled for bailout vote
KW

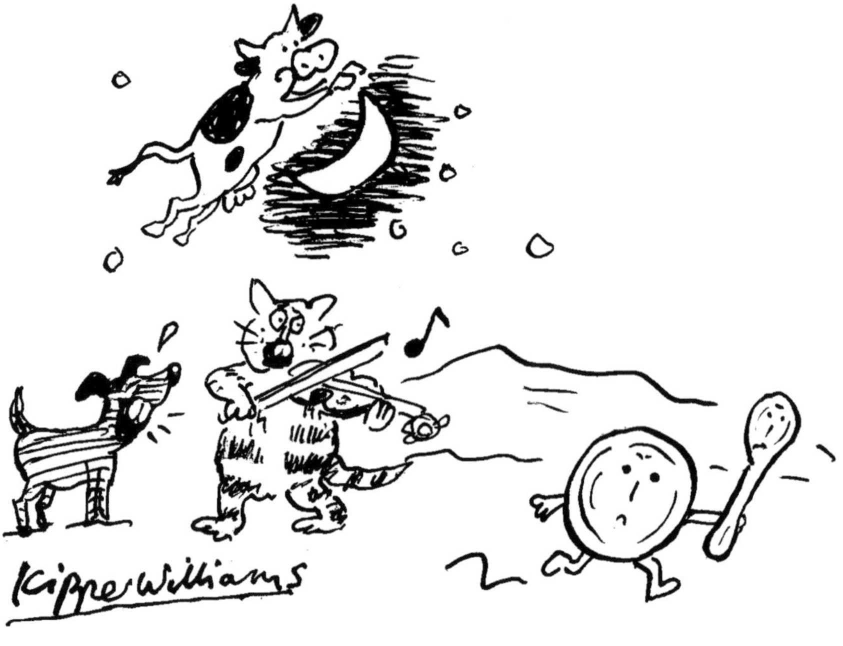
Kipper Williams

'Don't laugh – they're running away to Syria.'

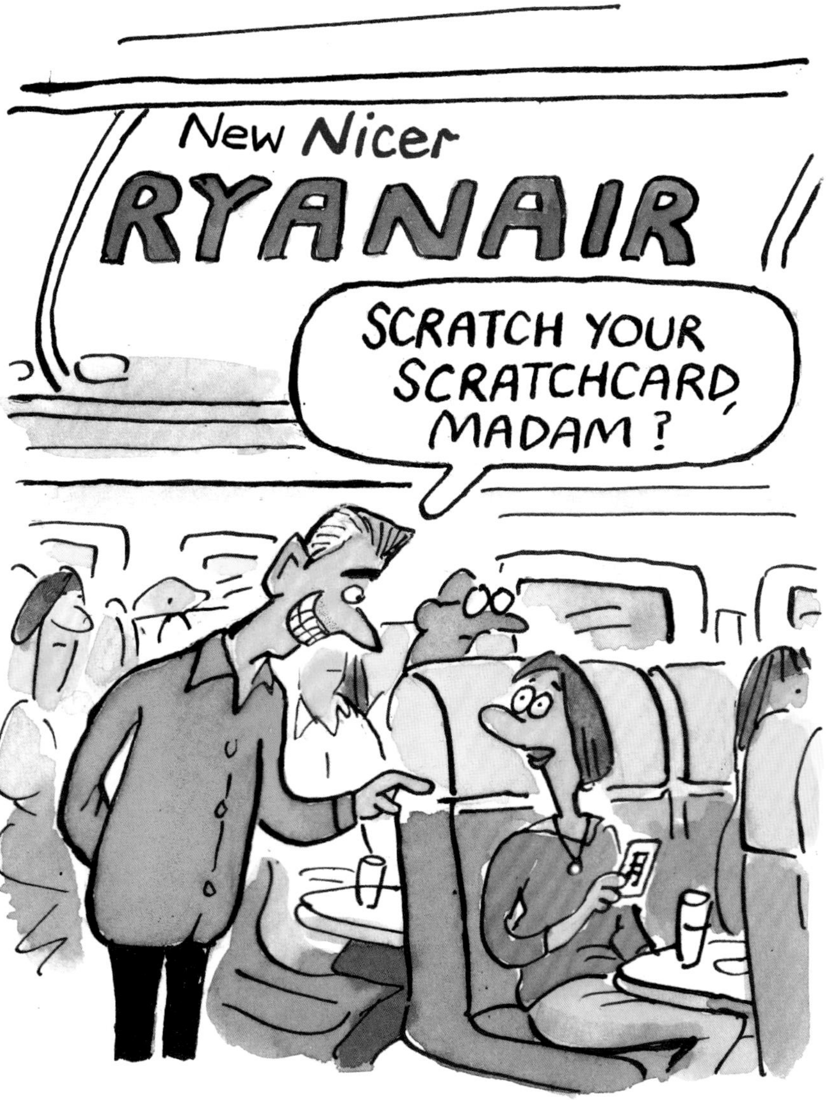
New Nicer
RYANAIR
SCRATCH YOUR SCRATCHCARD, MADAM?

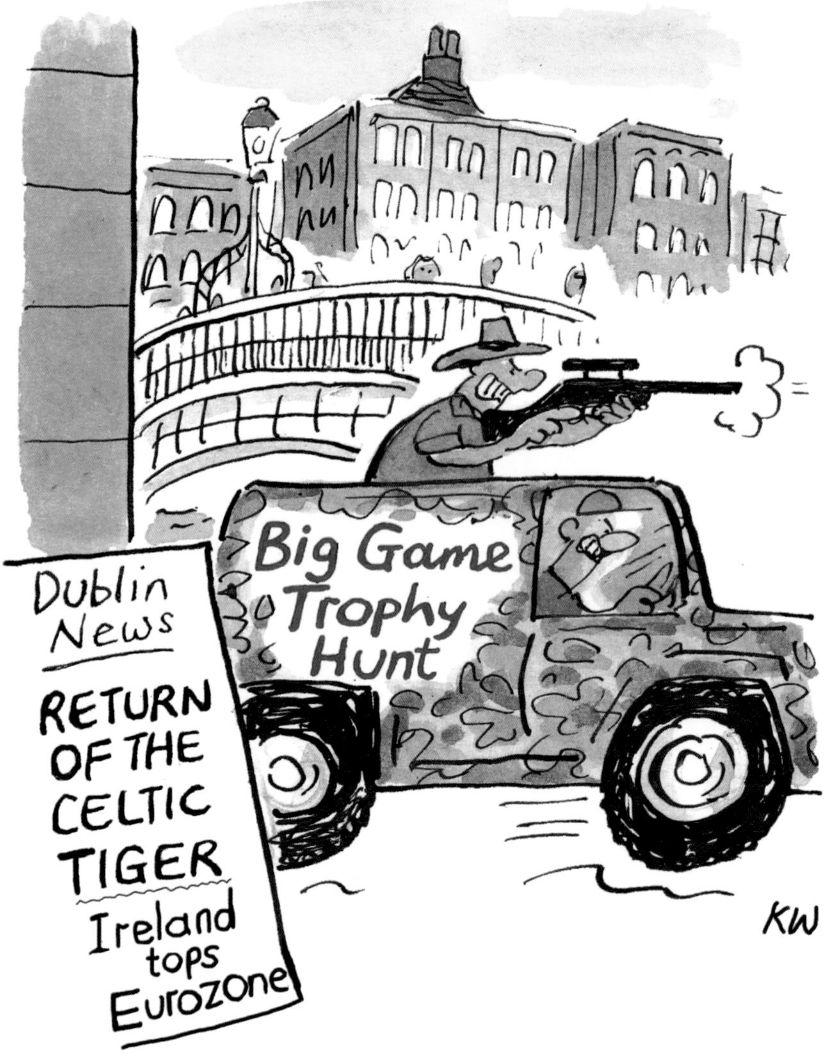
Big Game
Trophy
Hunt
Dublin
News
RETURN
OF THE
CELTIC
TIGER
Ireland
tops
Eurozone
KW

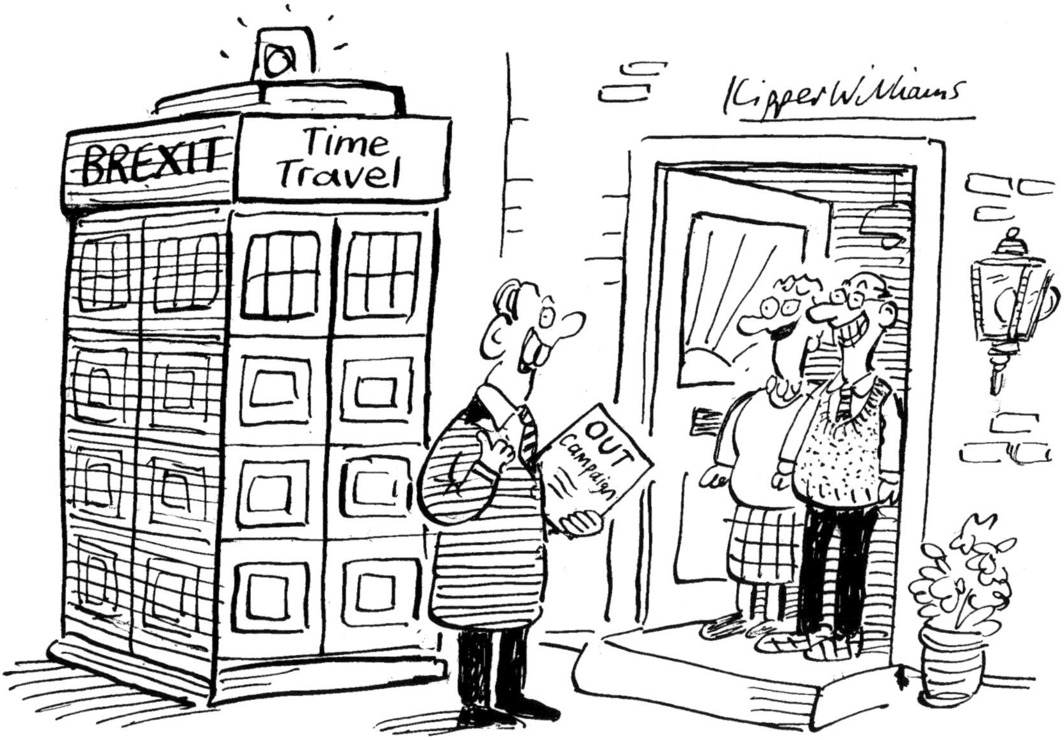
BREXIT
Time Travel
OUT Campaign
Kipper Williams

'It'll whisk you back to the sepia-tinted 1950s'

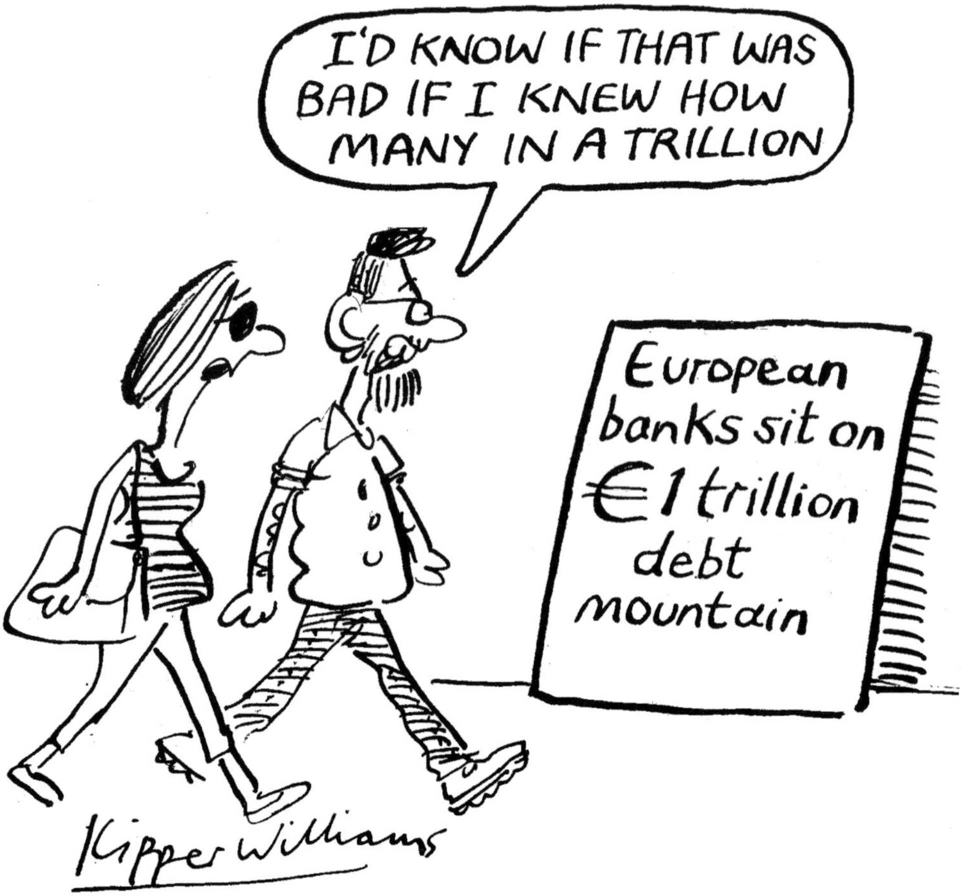
I'D KNOW IF THAT WAS BAD IF I KNEW HOW MANY IN A TRILLION
European banks sit on €1 trillion debt mountain
Kipper Williams

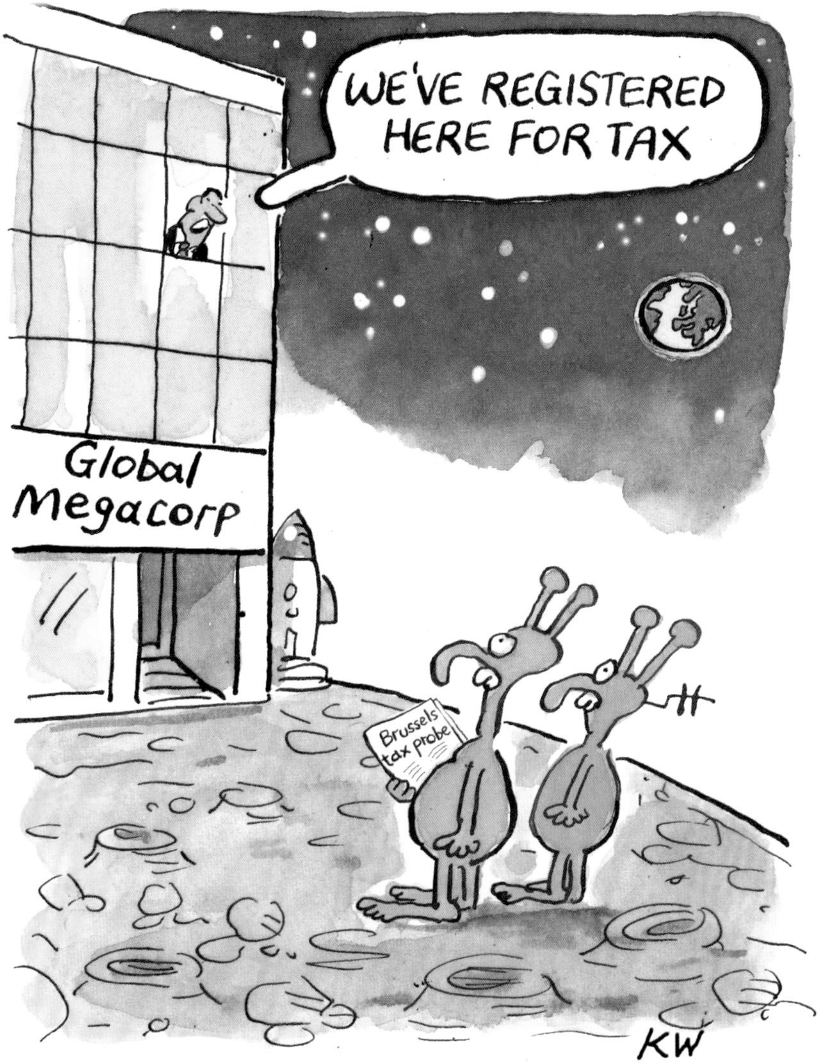
WE'VE REGISTERED HERE FOR TAX
Global Megacorp
Brussels tax probe
KW

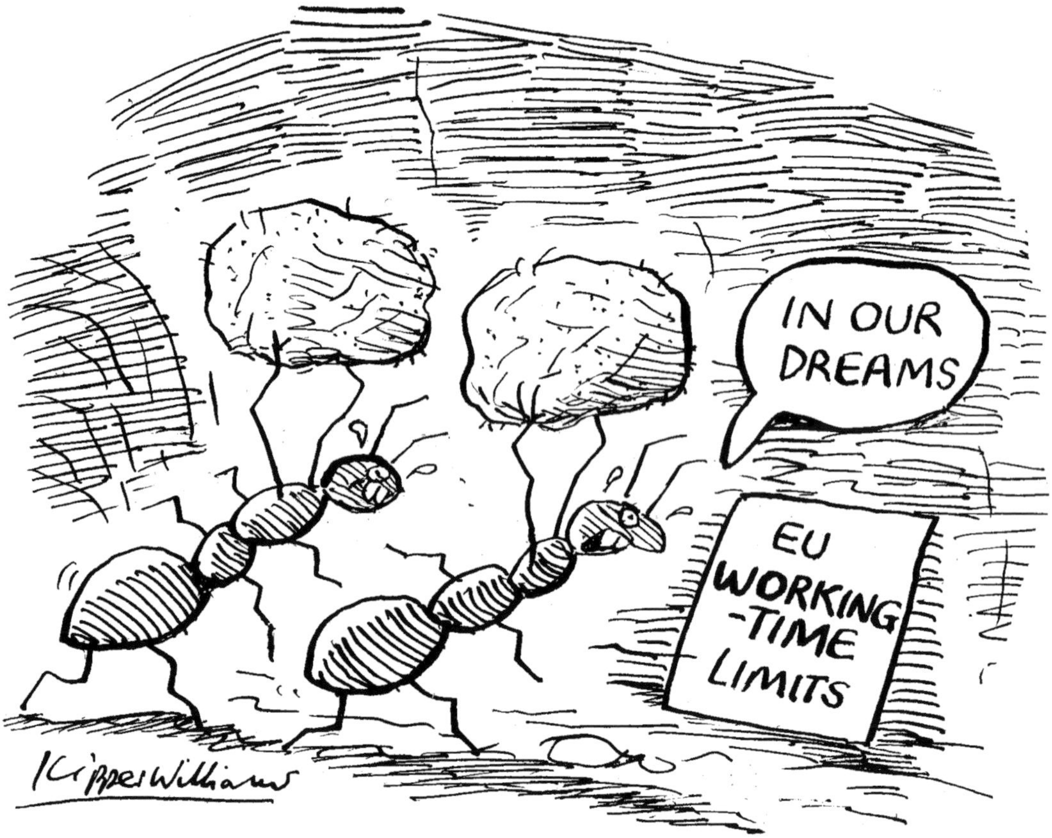
IN OUR DREAMS
EU WORKING-TIME LIMITS
KipperWilliams

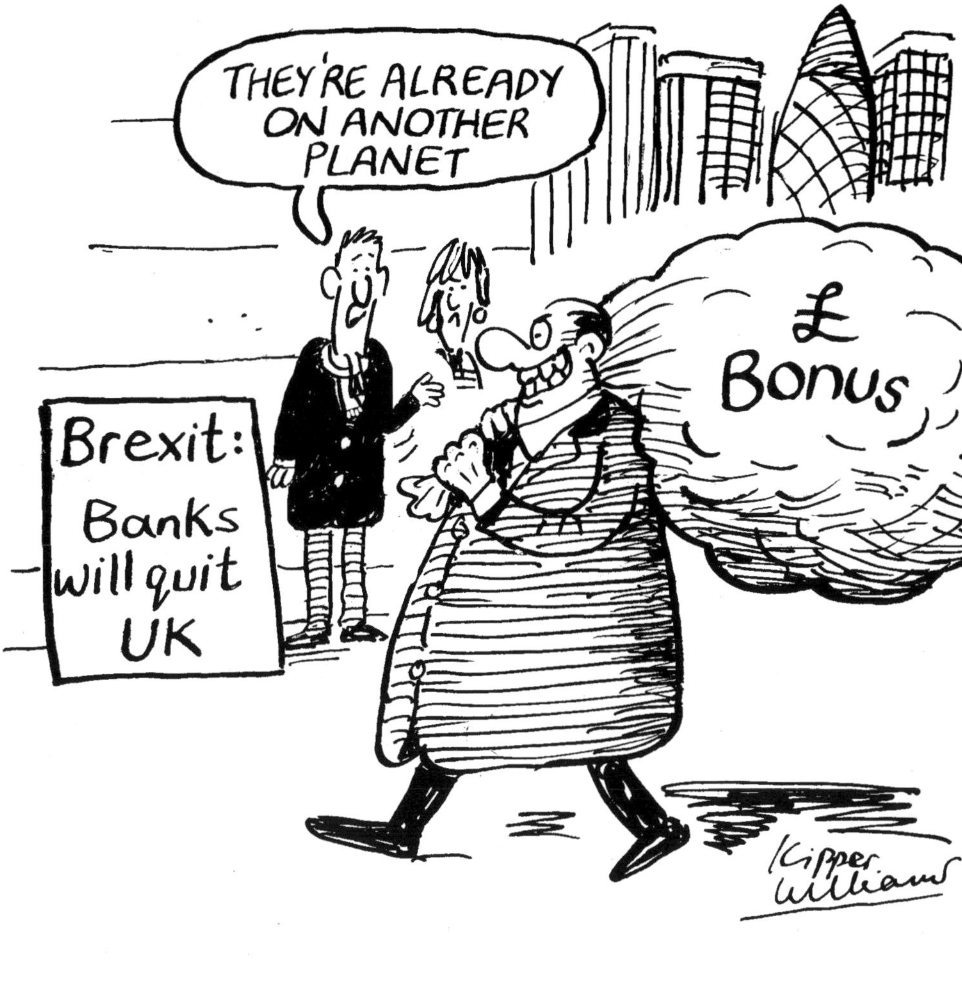
THEY'RE ALREADY ON ANOTHER PLANET
Brexit: Banks will quit UK
£ Bonus
Kipper Williams

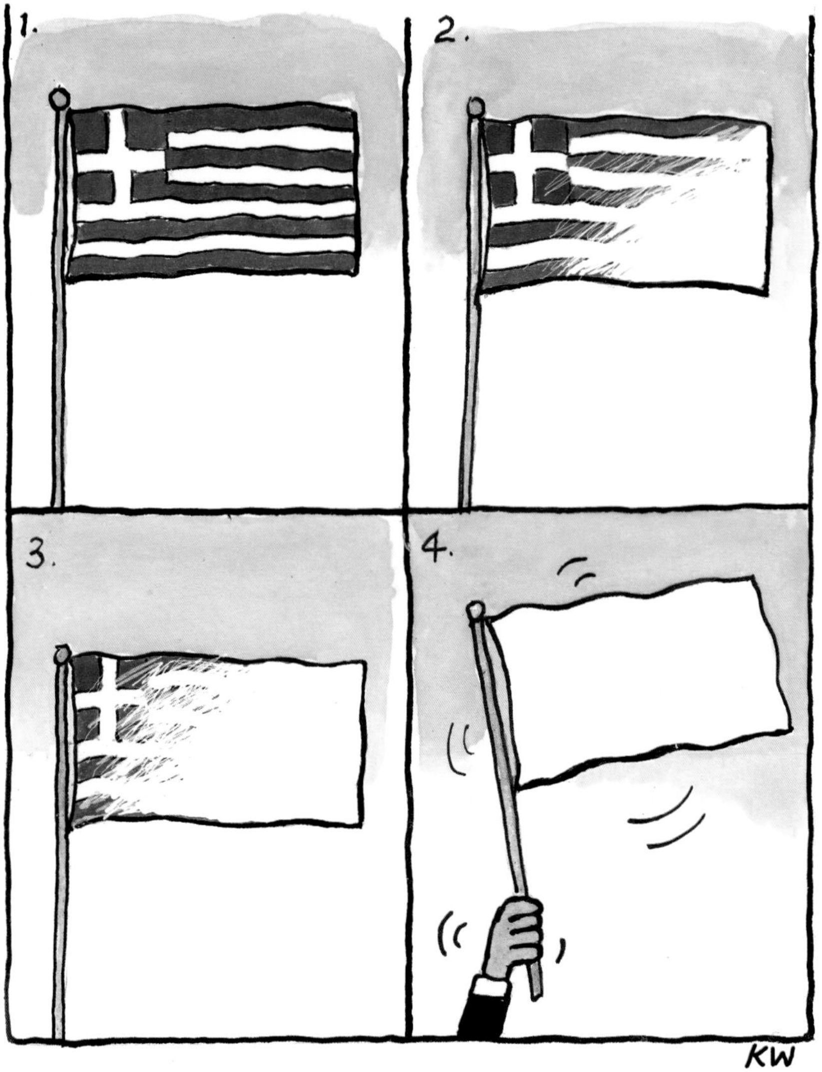
1.
2.
3.
4.
KW

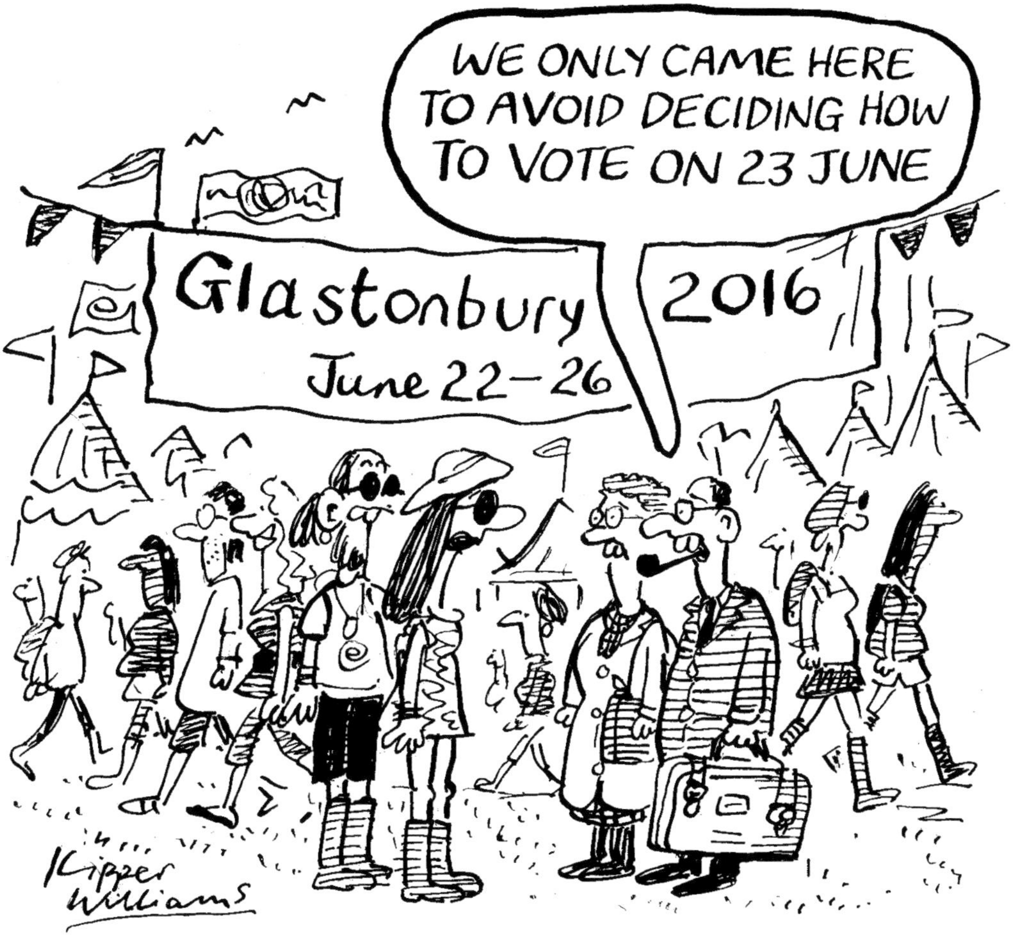
WE ONLY CAME HERE TO AVOID DECIDING HOW TO VOTE ON 23 JUNE
Glastonbury 2016
June 22–26
Kipper Williams

**BENDY
iPhone 6**

**BENDY
EU rules**

EU rules

KW

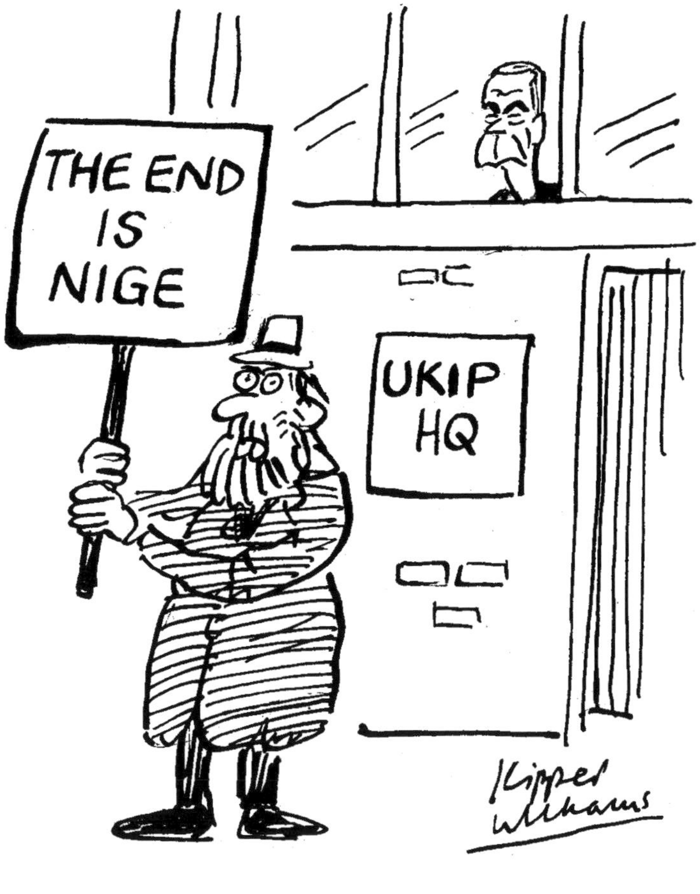
THE END IS NIGE
UKIP HQ
Kipper Williams

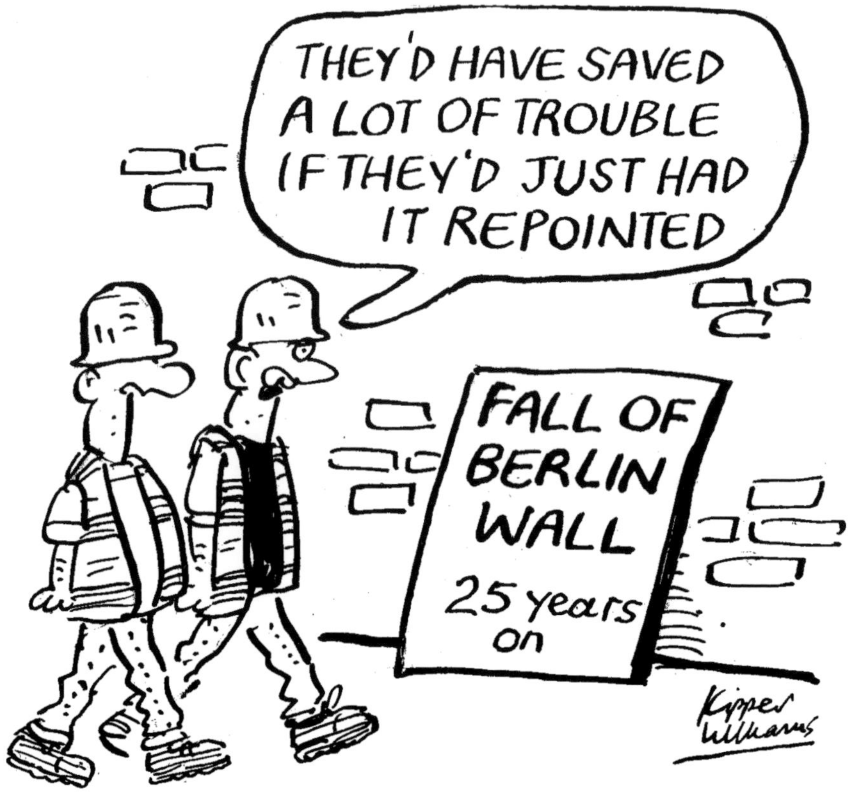
THEY'D HAVE SAVED A LOT OF TROUBLE IF THEY'D JUST HAD IT REPOINTED
FALL OF BERLIN WALL
25 years on
Kipper Williams

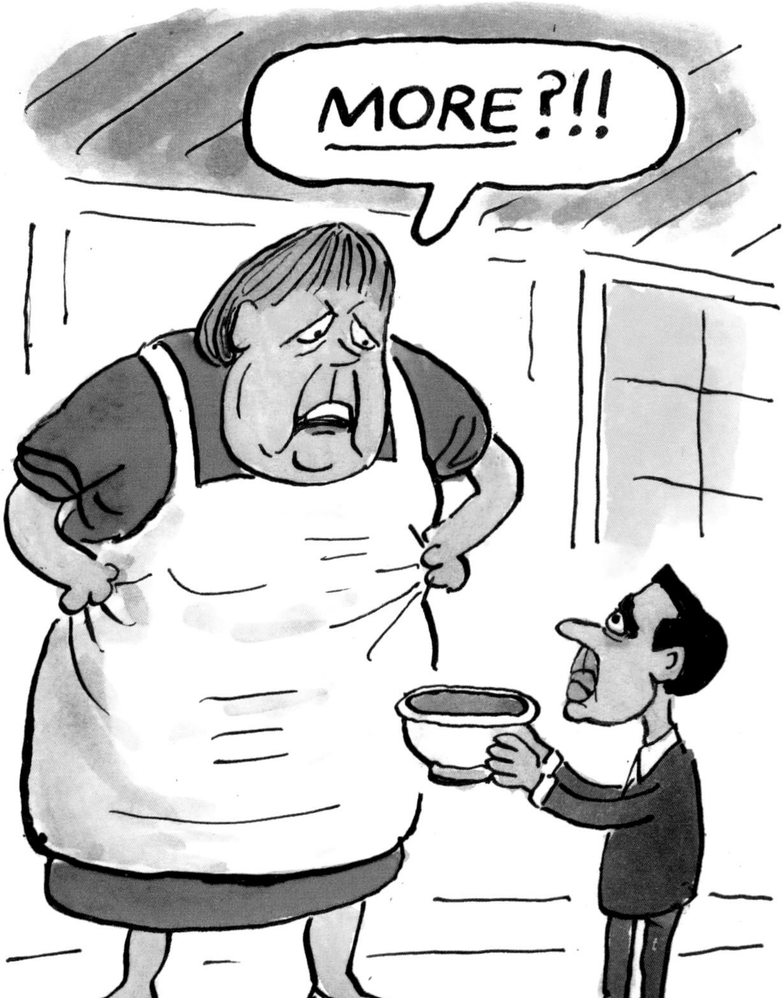
MORE?!!
KW

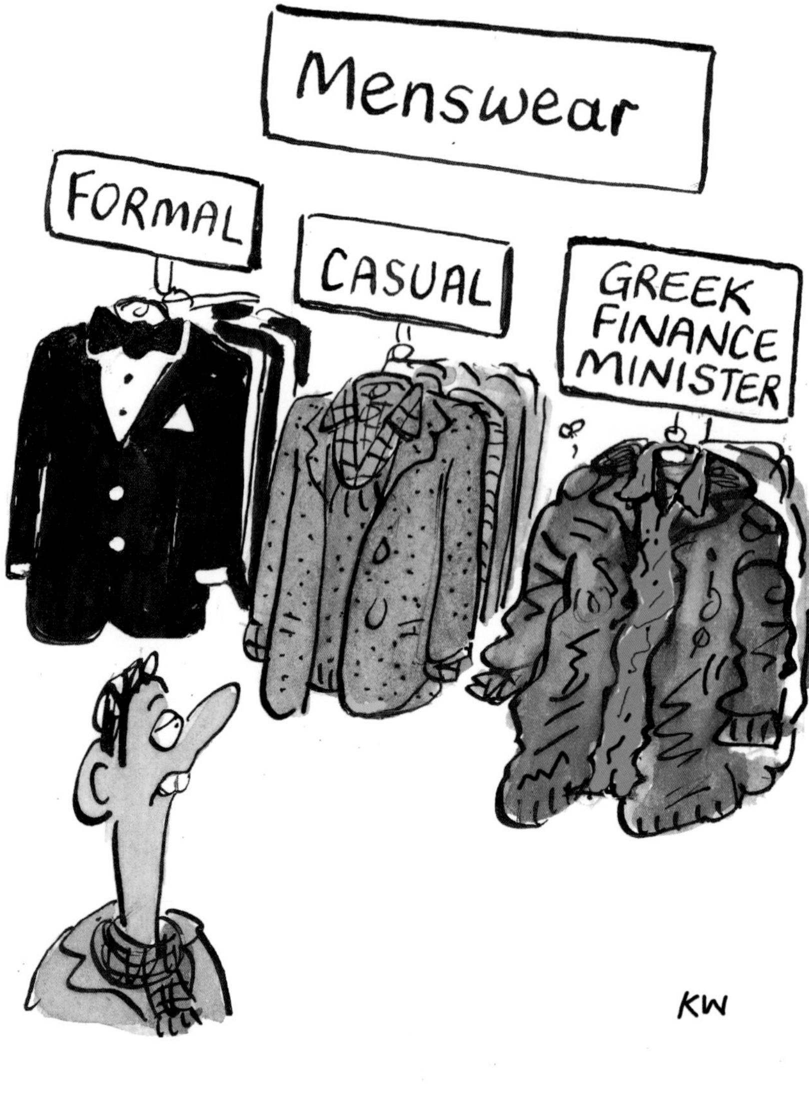
Menswear
FORMAL
CASUAL
GREEK FINANCE MINISTER
KW

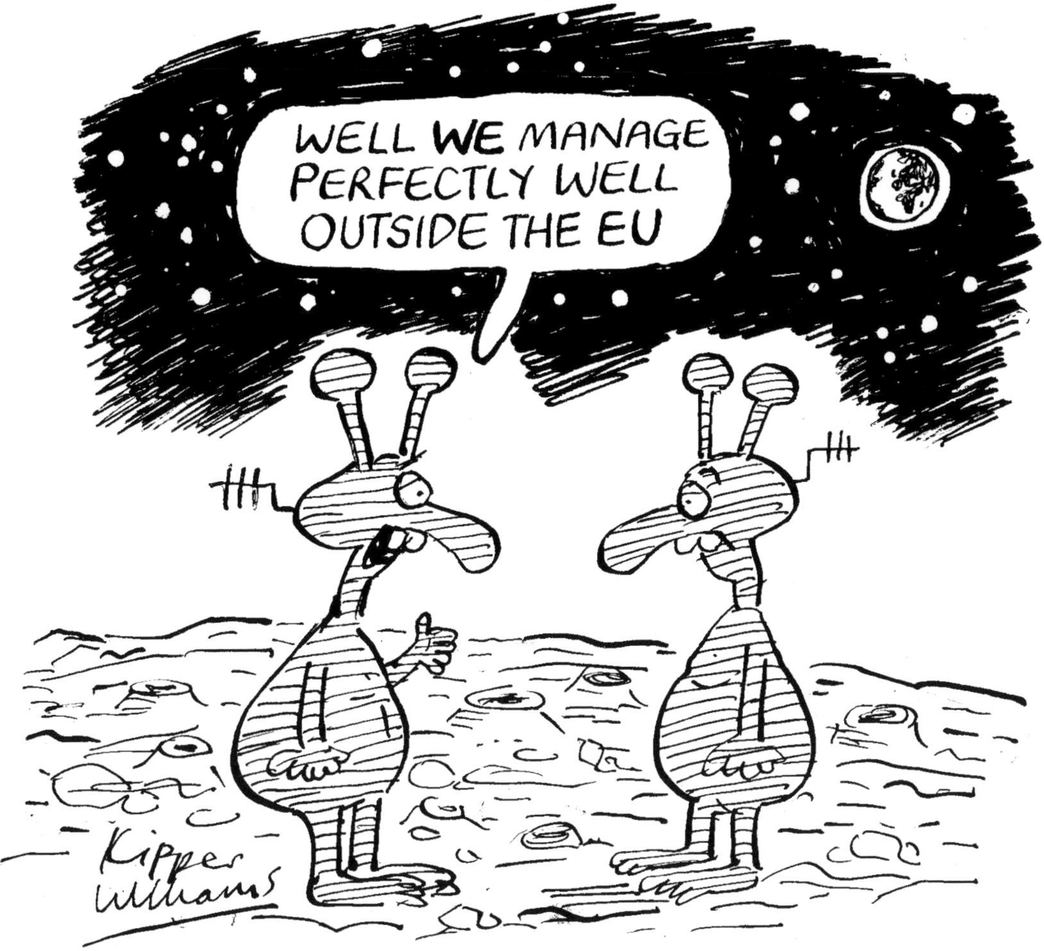
WELL WE MANAGE PERFECTLY WELL OUTSIDE THE EU
Kipper Williams

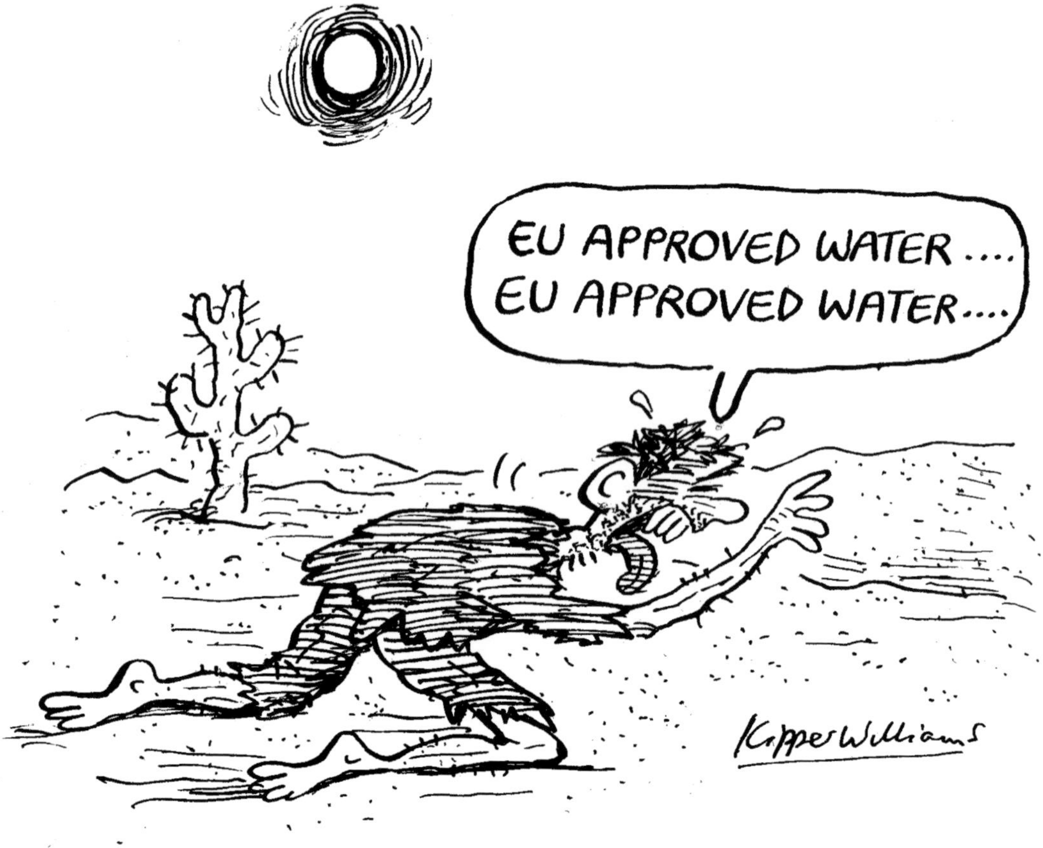
EU APPROVED WATER....
EU APPROVED WATER....
KipperWilliams

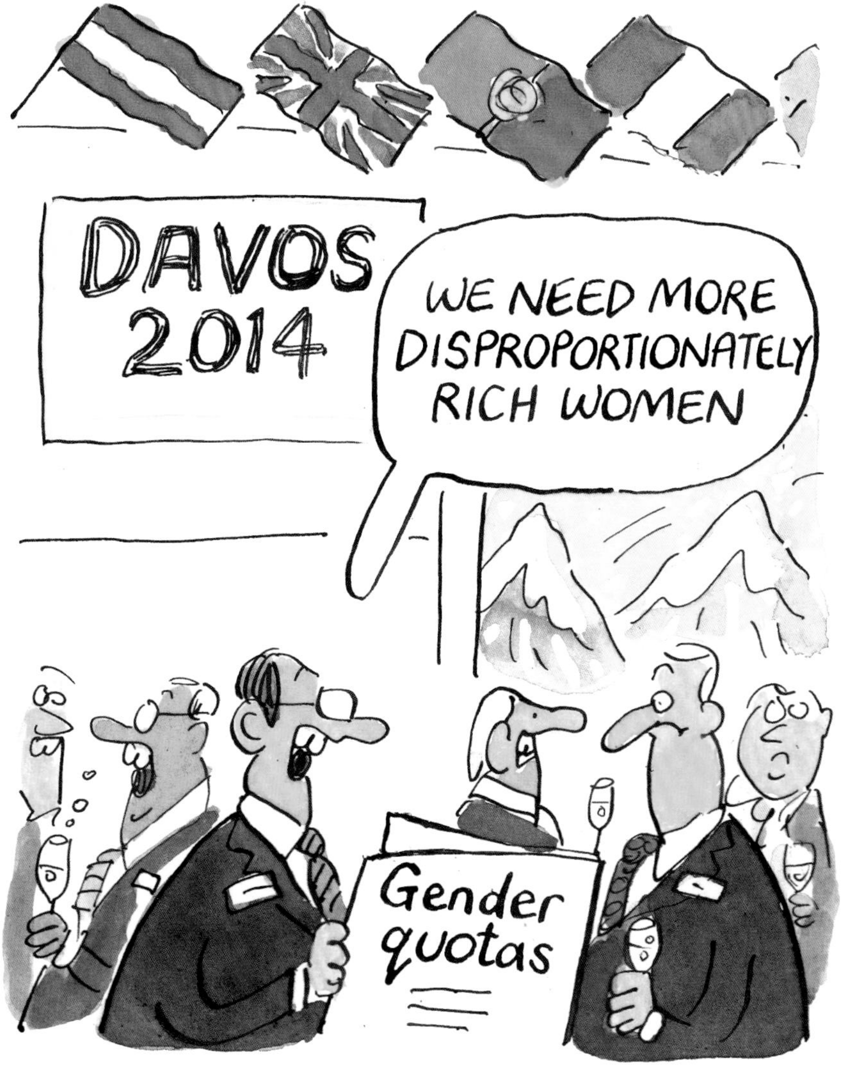
DAVOS
2014
WE NEED MORE
DISPROPORTIONATELY
RICH WOMEN
Gender
quotas

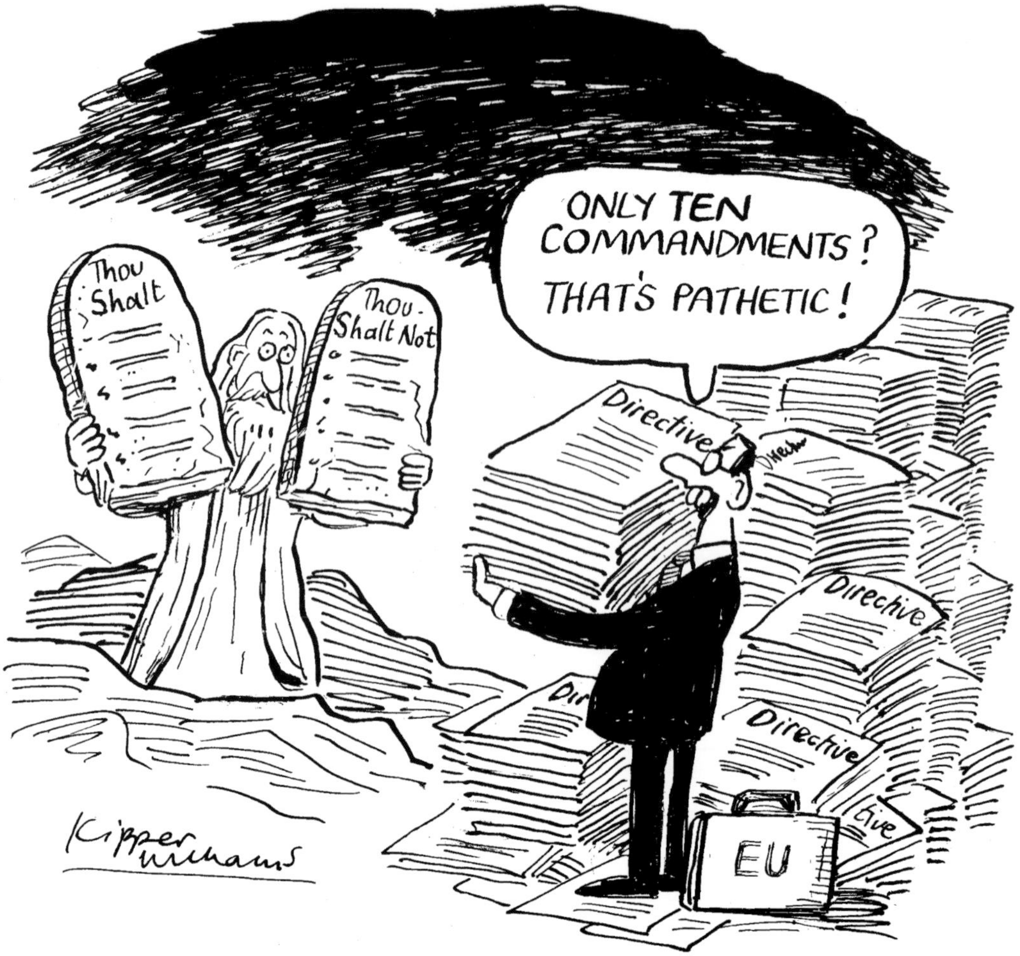
ONLY TEN COMMANDMENTS? THAT'S PATHETIC!
Thou Shalt
Thou Shalt Not
Directive
Directive
Directive
EU
Kipper Williams

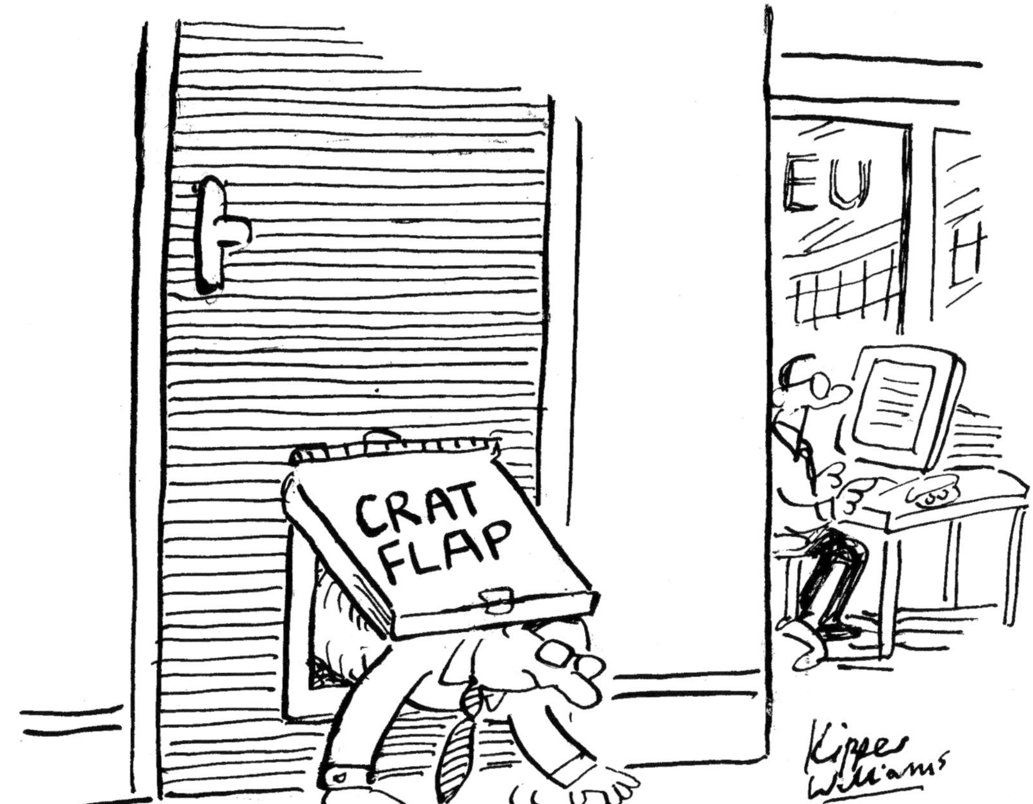
EU
CRAT
FLAP
Kipper
Williams

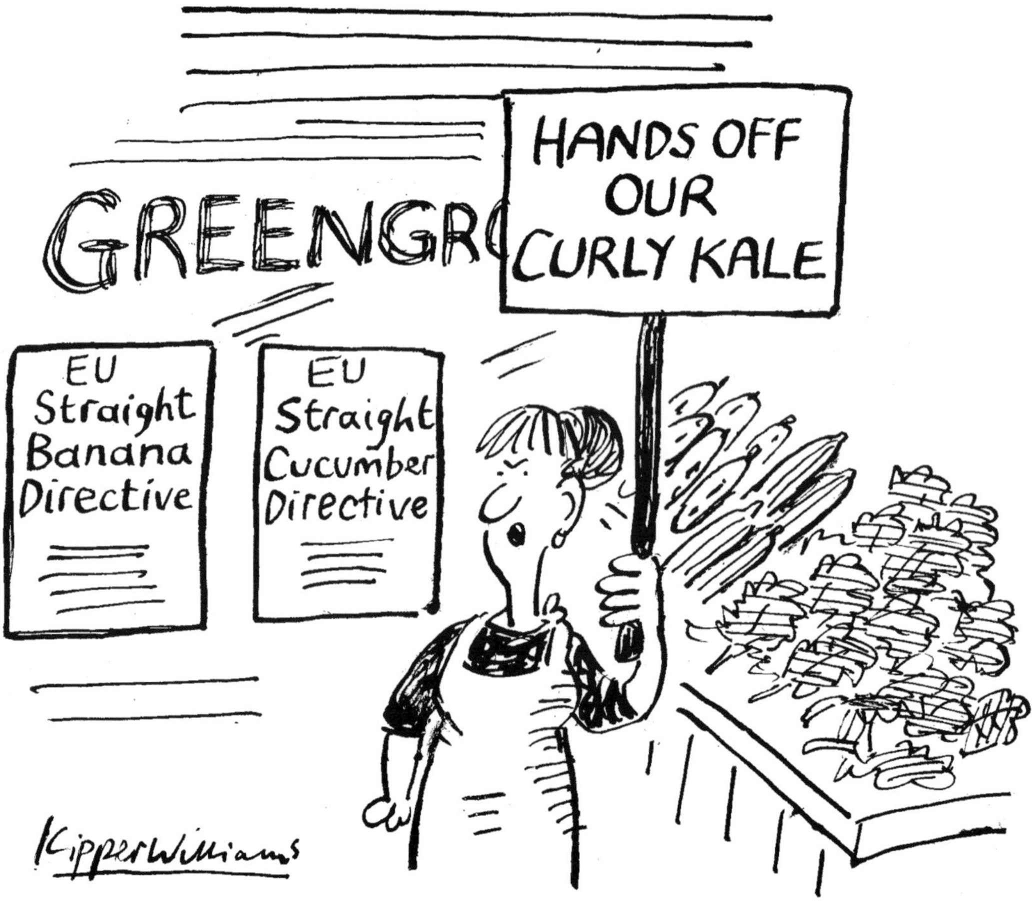
GREENGR
HANDS OFF OUR CURLY KALE
EU Straight Banana Directive
EU Straight Cucumber Directive
KipperWilliams

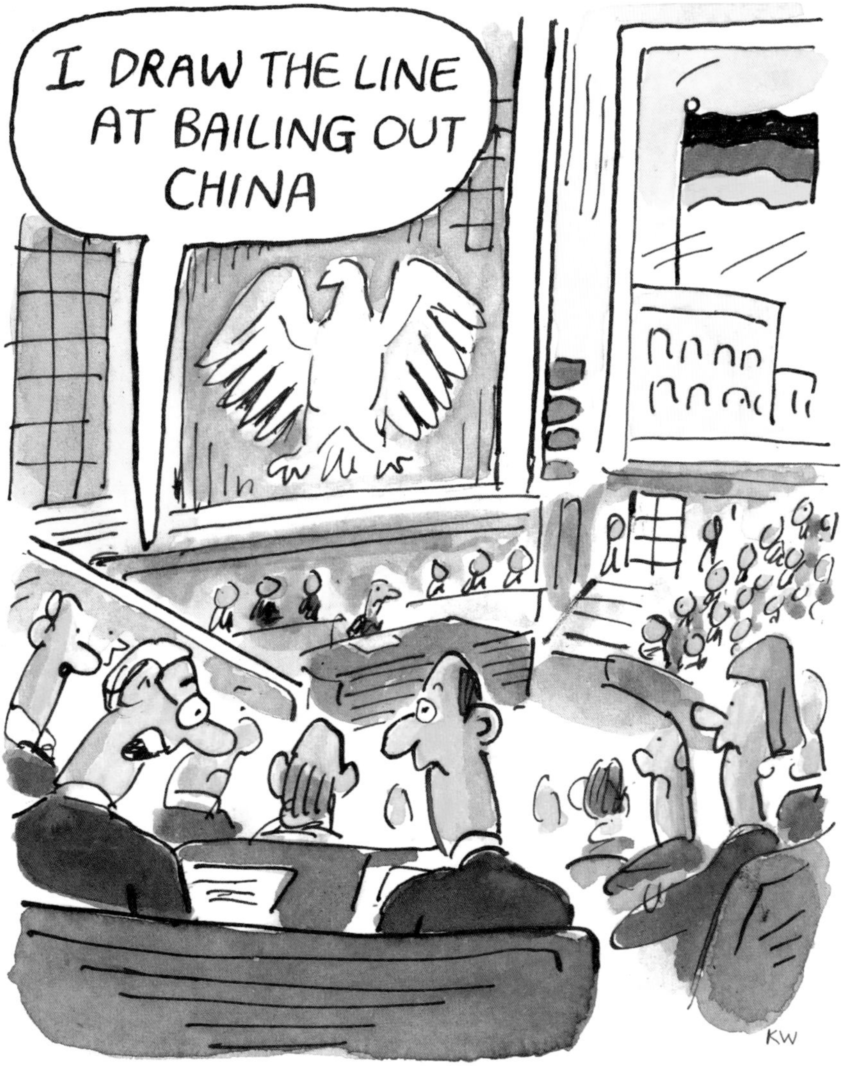
I DRAW THE LINE AT BAILING OUT CHINA
KW

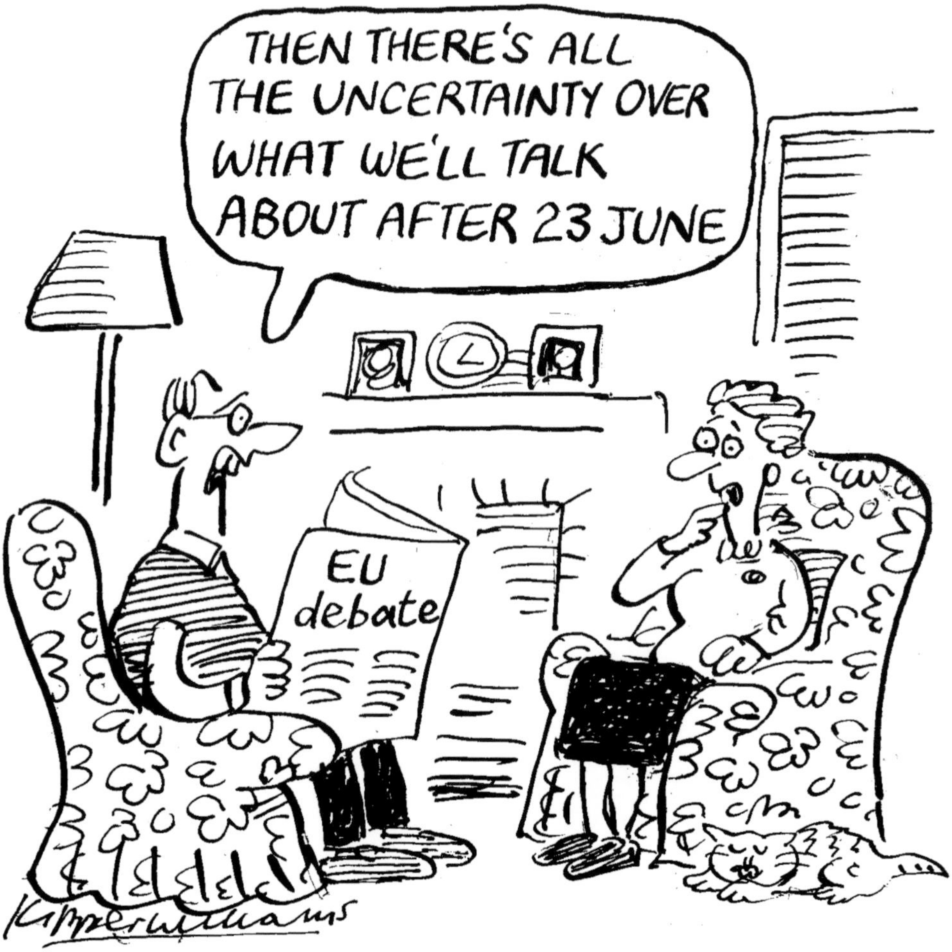
THEN THERE'S ALL THE UNCERTAINTY OVER WHAT WE'LL TALK ABOUT AFTER 23 JUNE
EU debate
Kipper Williams

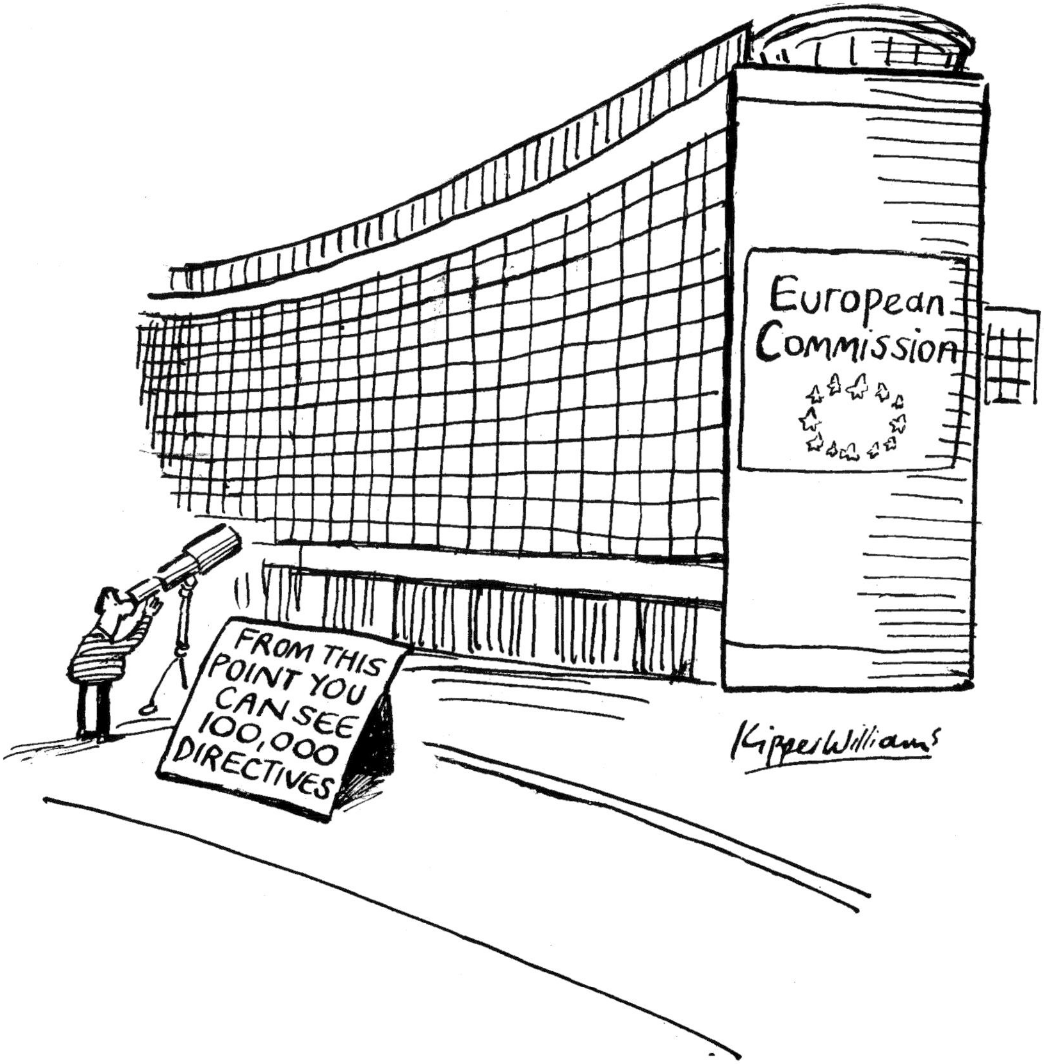

European
Commission
FROM THIS POINT YOU CAN SEE 100,000 DIRECTIVES
KipperWilliams

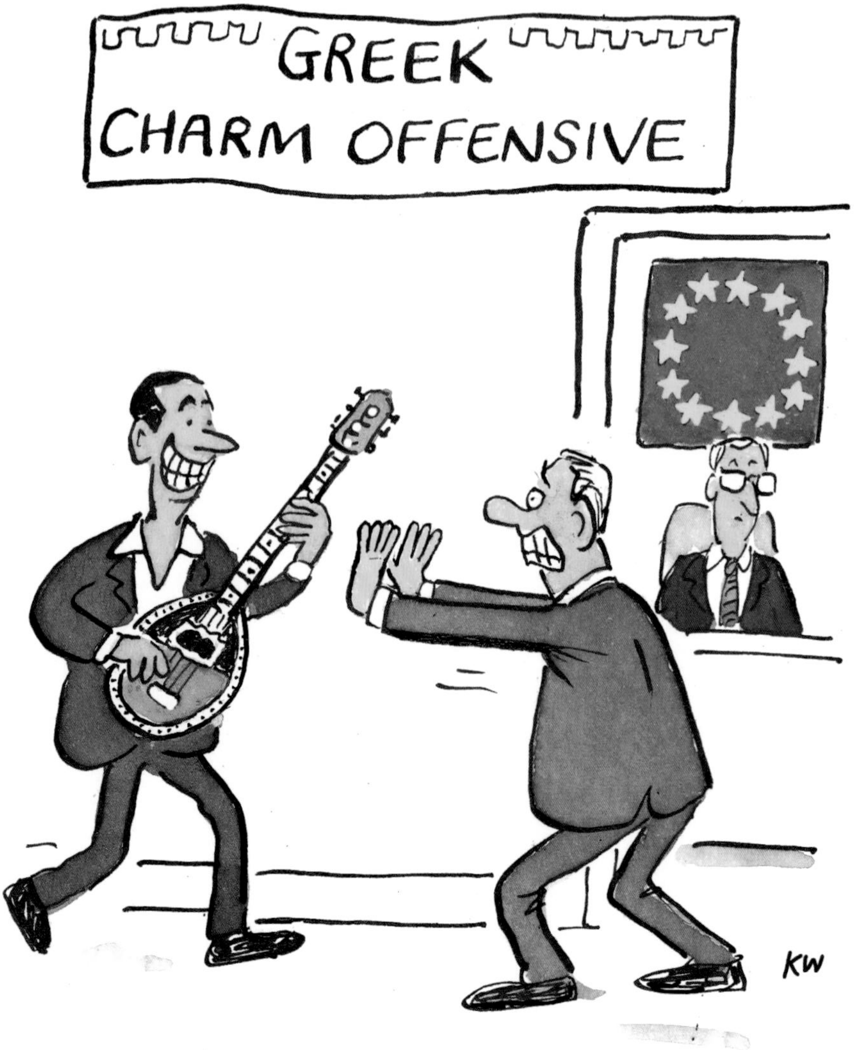
GREEK
CHARM OFFENSIVE
KW